Murder in Neighbourhood Watch

A Thriller

Stewart Burke

SAMUELFRENCH-LONDON.CO.UK
SAMUELFRENCH.COM

Copyright © 1990 by Aileen Burke and Leone Stewart
All Rights Reserved

MURDER IN NEIGHBOURHOOD WATCH is fully protected under the copyright laws of the British Commonwealth, including Canada, the United States of America, and all other countries of the Copyright Union. All rights, including professional and amateur stage productions, recitation, lecturing, public reading, motion picture, radio broadcasting, television and the rights of translation into foreign languages are strictly reserved.

ISBN 978-0-573-11290-4

www.samuelfrench-london.co.uk

www.samuelfrench.com

For Amateur Production Enquiries

United Kingdom and World excluding North America

plays@SamuelFrench-London.co.uk

020 7255 4302/01

Each title is subject to availability from Samuel French,

depending upon country of performance.

CAUTION: Professional and amateur producers are hereby warned that *MURDER IN NEIGHBOURHOOD WATCH* is subject to a licensing fee. Publication of this play does not imply availability for performance. Both amateurs and professionals considering a production are strongly advised to apply to the appropriate agent before starting rehearsals, advertising, or booking a theatre. A licensing fee must be paid whether the title is presented for charity or gain and whether or not admission is charged.

The professional rights in this play are controlled by Film Rights Ltd in Association with Laurence Fitch Ltd, 11 Pandora Road, London, NW6 1TS.

No one shall make any changes in this title for the purpose of production. No part of this book may be reproduced, stored in a retrieval system, or transmitted in any form, by any means, now known or yet to be invented, including mechanical, electronic, photocopying, recording, videotaping, or otherwise, without the prior written permission of the publisher. No one shall upload this title, or part of this title, to any social media websites.

The right of Stewart Burke to be identified as author of this work has been asserted by him in accordance with Section 77 of the Copyright, Designs and Patents Act 1988

CHARACTERS

Andrew Wingate
Sandra Coburn
Bruce Coburn
Joe Lipton
Ann Wingate
Chief Detective Inspector Parry-Jones-Evans
Melody

The action of the play takes place in Ann and Andrew Wingate's living-room

ACT I   SCENE 1   A Friday in November. Late evening
          SCENE 2   Saturday. Midday

ACT II   SCENE 1   Monday evening. 6 p.m.
          SCENE 2   Later that night

Time—the present

ACT I

Scene 1

The living-room in Ann and Andrew Wingate's home. A Friday in November. Late evening

In the back wall C, *an archway leads to a partly seen staircase* L *and opposite,* R, *the front door (unseen) part of a carpeted hall.* DR *a diamond-paned window looks out to the road, with a large potted plant on the sill. A glass patio door* UL *leads into the garden. A plain door* DL *leads to the kitchen*

The comfortably furnished room has a settee, two armchairs, a coffee table and a large fitment on the back wall LC *containing drinks, glasses, a record player, books, a hook for car keys and a lamp. There are a drawer and cupboard below. There is a desk* DR *with a telephone and lamp on it, and a swivel chair by it. Two upright chairs, one by the kitchen door and one in the hall space*

When the CURTAIN *rises, the room is spattered with mangled newspapers. Cuttings and scissors are on the settee. A tray on the coffee table holds the remains of a Chinese take-away meal. Woman's clothes—a long black skirt, a glitzy jacket, gloves, blonde wig—are on the chair by the kitchen door. A shoulder bag hangs by its strap over the back of the same chair. There is a large red file on top of the desk. Classical music is playing*

Andrew, wearing a track suit, enters from the kitchen, carrying a mug of coffee. He pauses C, *looks at his wrist-watch, sips the coffee then puts down the mug on the table and collects the cuttings and scissors from the settee. He goes to the desk, putting on the light there, and clips the cuttings into the file. He collects the clothes from the chair and takes them to the settee. He forgets the handbag*

Loud knocking on the front door. He looks towards archway but doesn't move. The knocking is repeated

Sandra (*off, calling through the letter-box*) Andrew, it's me—Sandra. I know you're in, I saw the lights. Open the door, please. It's urgent.
Andrew (*moving reluctantly to the archway*) I was going to shower and turn in. Won't the morning do?
Sandra (*off*) No, I must see you now. I need your help and I wouldn't worry you this late if it weren't important.
Andrew All right, hang on a minute.

He goes into fast action. He collects the clothes and stuffs them into the fitment cupboard, closing the door (forgetting the handbag)

Sandra (*off*) Oh, hurry up, it's freezing out here.

Satisfied he has hidden the "evidence" he goes into the hall to open the door

(*Off*) Oh, bless you. I couldn't think who to ask and then I saw your lights and thought: "There's one person who'll come to my rescue."

Sandra enters, followed by Andrew, who puts on the main lights

Andrew What's the trouble?

Sandra I've got the most agonizing toothache.

Andrew I'm sorry. (*He turns off the music*)

Sandra It's driving me crazy. I think the filling's fallen out, caused by the steak we had for supper. I'll have that butcher for mincemeat, selling tough best rump and charging the earth. He ought to be shown up. (*She sits on the settee, uninvited*) No competition in this village, that's the trouble. They get away with murder!

Andrew I'm not a dentist, Sandra, so how can I help?

Sandra Ann used to keep toothache tincture, mostly for Jason. I thought it might still be here.

Andrew I've never seen it.

Sandra Perhaps in her first-aid box. Have a look, be a good Samaritan. This brute is really giving me hell, I know I won't sleep a wink and Bruce is no help; he's out as usual.

Andrew I don't even know where the first-aid box is. Try a couple of aspirins.

Sandra I have and they've done absolutely nothing, except give me a headache.

Andrew Hot salt's a remedy. My grandmother used to swear by it.

Sandra When is Ann coming home?

Andrew Nothing definite.

Sandra It's a long time to be away. Three months, isn't it?

Andrew Something like that.

Sandra I miss her. I expect you do, too.

Andrew Naturally, but really Sandra, I must——

Sandra Not easy, fending for yourself.

Andrew I manage.

Sandra (*looking around her*) Yes, so I see. A house slips when it isn't cared for.

Andrew It's late and I really would like to turn in, so if you don't mind——

Sandra Yes, you must get tired with so much to do. It's not right, a man expected to care for himself as well as doing a full-time job. You can always come over to us for a meal, you know that. I've said it often enough.

Andrew Thank you, but I have a good lunch at the school.

Sandra School dinners, huh! My daughter says the cabbage is a disgrace and as for the tapioca pudding—frog spawn.

Andrew Good-night, Sandra.

Sandra All you have to do is give me the wink and I'll see you're decently nourished, least I can do. Ann would expect me to keep an eye on you.

Andrew And you're doing that very thoroughly.
Sandra I do pot roasts, chicken on the spit and steak. (*She rubs her face*) To my cost. I'll have to go to the dentist tomorrow and my man's away so I'll have to see his partner. That's awkward, as he doesn't know my mouth.
Andrew He soon will.

Pause

Sandra Why don't you have a woman?
Andrew What?
Sandra To clean for you. This place is a shambles, you must admit. When was this carpet last vacuumed?
Andrew It doesn't need it.
Sandra Well, I couldn't live with it myself.
Andrew You don't have to.
Sandra And why do you eat in here when you have a perfectly good kitchen dinette?
Andrew I like to listen to music.
Sandra Yes, I suppose it takes your mind off what you're eating. Ann promised to send me a postcard, you know, and I haven't received it. How could she stay away so long and forget us all?
Andrew She's having a well deserved holiday with her parents——
Sandra A wife's place——
Andrew Is where she wants to be. And right now Ann wants to be in New Zealand.
Sandra If you were my husband I wouldn't chance it.
Andrew Chance what?
Sandra You're a very dishy man, Andrew; oh, very dishy. The first time I saw you I thought: "Wow, why didn't I have the luck to marry him?" Instead I got Bruce.
Andrew And Bruce will be wondering where you are.
Sandra I told you. He's out. No idea where. If I didn't know him better I'd say it's another woman, but sex isn't his strong suit. No, hardly any interest there. The men you can trust usually aren't worth having. Oh, not that I'm saying a word against Bruce.
Andrew Aren't you?
Sandra No, he's a good husband and father... sometimes. It's just that he's so—unexciting. Predictable.
Andrew No man is wholly predictable.
Sandra Oh, you're not. No-one could ever guess what you're thinking or doing for that matter. A bit of a mystery and that makes you all the more fascinating.
Andrew (*going to the archway*) I'll see you across the road.
Sandra Tris told me the other girls at your school think you're macho. That's how you're able to keep discipline so well. When she heard you were going to take the music lessons she insisted on joining the class.
Andrew Please, Sandra, go home.
Sandra I'm telling you, you wouldn't have far to look if Ann has left you.
Andrew Ann has not left me!

Sandra Then why stay away so long? I always think a wife has lost interest in the marriage if she doesn't worry about her husband's supper.
Andrew (*clapping a hand to his head*) Oh, my God!
Sandra Ann should be here to take care of you. We never know what mischief a man will get up to when he's deserted. (*Gasping*) Oh, not you, Andrew. A headmaster has to be above suspicion, like Caesar's wife.
Andrew Do me a favour, Sandra.
Sandra (*jumping up*) Anything, Andrew, anything at all.
Andrew Then go home!
Sandra I've only just got here. Besides, I don't think you should be on your own so much.

He begins to collect the newspapers and stacks them in the waste-paper basket by the desk

Andrew I like being on my own.
Sandra It's not healthy. You'll get depressed.
Andrew I am depressed. Very, very depressed this minute.
Sandra I can see you are and I'm trying to cheer you up.
Andrew I don't believe this.
Sandra Then you should because if it's one thing I am, it's a loyal friend and neighbour and if people start talking about someone——
Andrew About me? Do they talk about me?
Sandra About anyone if they get the chance. At my last coffee morning I said straight out: "Now girls, let's make this amicable. No rubbing neighbours and friends in the dust. I don't want my house soiled."

Andrew finishes his coffee

Oh, thirsty, are you? Come to think of it so am I.
Andrew Alcohol is bad for toothache.
Sandra It could help me to sleep, calm me down. We're out of Scotch across the road. Bruce forgot to order any.

Andrew, resigned, pours a drink for her

I'm being a nuisance. Oh, yes I am, don't try to deny it. When I've had my little drink I'll go home, that's a promise and you know me, I never break a promise.

The phone rings. Sandra goes to lift the receiver on the desk

Andrew (*spinning round*) Leave it!
Sandra I was trying to be helpful——
Andrew (*shouting*) Leave it, Sandra, leave it!
Sandra All right, all right, you don't have to shout.

Andrew joins her, thrusting the glass into her hand

Andrew Drink it and then go home.
Sandra Aren't you going to answer it?

He snatches up the receiver

Andrew (*curtly on the phone*) You have the wrong number! (*He slams down the receiver*)
Sandra How do you know it was a wrong number? You didn't give them a chance to speak. It might have been anyone. Urgent even.
Andrew It was a wrong number.
Sandra How can you be sure?
Andrew I am sure.
Sandra It might have been Ann from New Zealand. It's day-time there, isn't it? She could have been calling to say when she's coming home. Or if she's *not* coming home.

Shaken, Andrew pours himself a drink

If you don't mind my saying so, Andrew, you have been behaving very oddly of late. I was only saying to Bruce this morning——
Andrew I am not interested in what you were saying to Bruce this morning or any other morning. I just want you to go home so I can lock up, shower and turn in. I'm very, very tired and, yes, you are being a nuisance.
Sandra (*settling back on the settee*) I'm not leaving while you're like this. I don't know what has upset you, yet something obviously has. You never used to be so rude and inhospitable.
Andrew My good manners have been stretched to breaking point tonight. I'm sorry, but I've had an unwelcome visitor.
Sandra Oh, really, who came round?
Andrew If you don't go home I may put my hands around your throat and throttle you!
Sandra You shouldn't joke about such matters.
Andrew Who's joking?
Sandra One murder is enough. We don't want another.

Pause

There's a new man down from Scotland Yard. Did you know?

Andrew shakes his head wearily

He's here to help the local police, so I've heard. They can certainly do with help. Nearly two weeks since that poor woman ... well, you'd think they'd have arrested someone by now. Bruce says I mustn't go into the woods alone day or night. He thinks the thug could strike again. Do you think he'll strike again, Andrew?
Andrew I don't know. (*He sits in the swivel chair and puts his head in his hands*)
Sandra Murder gets the district a bad name. Mrs Allan was saying at my last coffee morning that she and her husband were worried now that they might not get the price they want for their bungalow. Mind you, it makes you think you'd like to get away.
Andrew It does indeed. Right this minute I should like to get far, far away.
Sandra They say this Scotland Yard man is rather eccentric. Well, who cares so long as he gets results and catches that monster?

Pause

It's strange I haven't heard from Ann.
Andrew *I* have heard.
Sandra Yes, but then you'd say you had even if—oh, sorry, Andrew, it's this damned tooth, it's making me say things I shouldn't. In any case I'm a friend and the last thing I'd do is spread gossip and rumours, like some people. I mind my own business.

She obviously does not. Andrew rises and goes to the archway

Andrew Perhaps Ann kept the tincture in the bathroom cabinet. I'll look upstairs.
Sandra There's no rush. I haven't finished my drink yet.
Andrew Then finish it, please, while I look for the tincture.
Sandra (*jumping up and going to him*) I've offended you. Oh, yes, I have, don't try to deny it. I'm sure Ann hasn't met with any harm. I'm sure she'll walk in that door one of these fine days and then the gossipers can eat their words.
Andrew (*interested now*) What are their words?

She turns away, embarrassed

Tell me. Go on, tell me. Or shall I tell you? Andrew Wingate has disposed of his wife and buried her in the garden.
Sandra Don't say things like that.
Andrew Why not, Sandra? You listen eagerly to the twittering coffee morning cronies, but when I spell out the details of my crime you shudder in horror. Or is it excitement?

He looks into her face and she backs away

Sandra If you go on like this you'll make me nervous. I'll be afraid to come over here.
Andrew My wife told everyone she was going on holiday, then, mysteriously, a week before she was due to leave, she disappeared and hasn't been heard of since.
Sandra You said you had heard.
Andrew And you don't believe me, do you. Do you, Sandra?
Sandra All I said was it's strange Ann hasn't written to her friends, and when people don't hear they start ... well, thinking things.
Andrew Like: "I wonder if he's a mass murderer? First his poor wife and now Marion Ellis. Hardly a fit person to teach our children. Perhaps we should hound him out of the village." (*He swings away from her and finishes his drink*)
Sandra It's lack of calories. You're under-nourished and it's having a bad effect on your digestive system. (*She pauses by the table and flicks at the foil cartons*) Chinese-Bring-Home. I ask you—what's in there, bamboo shoots? If you're not careful, Andrew, you'll turn into a giant panda.
Andrew God, help me!
Sandra Men who go without regular food have bad hallucinations. I read that somewhere. I think it was *Reader's Digest*.

Andrew I have little taste for food but I may have acquired a taste for murder. And at any moment now there may be another victim.
Sandra If Ann were here you wouldn't be talking like this.
Andrew If Ann were here the rest of you wouldn't be sitting by the guillotine, waiting for the next head to roll. How's the knitting?
Sandra I don't listen to gossip. I don't.
Andrew Then how do you know what they're saying?
Sandra You can't help *hearing* things. Besides, I don't choose the people who come to my coffee mornings. I hold them for charity and so all are welcome. It stands to reason that when a murder happens in a village — well, people start to speculate. It isn't as if *I* doubt you, Andrew——
Andrew No?
Sandra No. There's enough evil and violence in the world without us all starting to doubt our neighbours and friends. It's all the publicity. You never know when you switch on the television if you'll see yourself walking down the village street.
Andrew Highlights a dull day, surely?
Sandra I don't know about that. Every woman here is afraid now.
Andrew But a handful are enjoying themselves, coffee mornings are thriving. People want to get together to mull it all over. We're news! Reporters hanging around, taking up the parking spaces, chewing their pencils, getting pissed in *The Black Swan*. We're also a peep show for the grisly minded. Why not give the family a treat, hop in the car, take a picnic, visit Bracken Woods, hear the birds singing *and know this is where Marion Ellis was brutally raped and murdered*!
Sandra (*hands over her ears*) Stop it, Andrew, stop it!
Andrew Why, are facts ugly when taken out of the context of a soap opera?
Sandra Perhaps I'd better go home. I'm getting deeper into hot water every time I open my mouth. Bruce is always telling me to watch what I say and I never seem to. He thinks I'm not very bright. (*She sniffs*) Forgive me, Andrew, if I've upset you. I didn't mean to. We're still friends, aren't we?
Andrew (*nodding*) I'll look upstairs for the tincture.
Sandra Thank you. I would be grateful.

He exits to the stairs

Sandra goes swiftly to the desk and looks at the cuttings file, avidly curious. She takes the tray from the coffee table out to the kitchen. Returning at once she pauses by the chair, seeing the handbag. She touches it. A knock at the front door. Sandra goes into the hall

(*Calling upstairs*) Someone at the door. Shall I answer it?
Andrew (*off*) Yes, please.
Sandra I can't think who it can be this late.

She exits to the door. Voices are heard off

(*Off*) Oh, it's you.

She returns to the hall and calls to Andrew

It's Bruce. (*She enters the room*)

Bruce enters the room. He is well wrapped up in a heavy overcoat

Bruce What the hell do you think you're doing here?

Sandra I've got toothache and a fat lot of good you are, disappearing off on your own for hours——

Bruce I got in and didn't know where you were. I've already called at "Marbella" and "Lyndhurst". I felt a right fool having to say you were out and had no idea where. You should have more sense than to come calling here at this time of night, especially when his wife's away.

Sandra He's harmless.

Bruce But neighbours' tongues aren't.

Sandra You're always saying we shouldn't care what people think. Anyway, I'm not his type, and I think he's got someone else.

Bruce Keep your voice down, woman.

Sandra Handbag over on that chair and not Ann's. She likes clutch bags.

Bruce Have you been pestering him?

Sandra Yes—for toothache tincture.

Bruce It doesn't matter what time of day or night it is you think nothing of barging in on the neighbours and annoying them.

Sandra He's lonely. He was glad of my company.

Bruce Don't kid yourself.

Sandra Some people appreciate me, even if you don't.

Andrew enters with a bottle of tincture

Andrew Good guess. Bathroom cabinet. Hallo, is this a search party, Bruce? If so, you're just in time to escort your wife home. She was on the point of leaving. I warned her you'd be anxious.

Sandra Not him. He's been out for hours.

Bruce I like to take a breather before turning in. Shifts the old headache, you know, Andrew. I've always had trouble with migraine. Pills don't help.

Sandra And nor do cigarettes; and it's my lungs that have to suffer with all that smoke ballooning around the house.

Bruce Stop nit-picking, will you? I'm sure Andrew isn't interested in my weak habits.

Sandra See, he admits it . . . forty a day and coughing his heart out. Well, I couldn't sleep at night if he wasn't fully insured.

Bruce Sorry about all this, Andrew, nothing worse than listening to other people's domestic trivia.

Andrew (*smiling and handing the tincture to Sandra*) There you are. I hope it helps.

Sandra Oh, thank you; yes, I'm sure it will.

Bruce I knew she hadn't gone far, leaving the front door wide open. We could have been stripped . . . I've spent a small fortune on security locks and then she does stupid things like that. No point in all this Neighbourhood Watch Scheme if you openly invite thieves——

Sandra That's right, blame me for everything.

Andrew If your front door is still open, hadn't you better——

Act I, Scene 2

Bruce Yes, we're going. Sorry again about all this.
Andrew Parent–teacher meeting on Monday evening, Sandra——
Sandra I'll be there. I doubt if *he* will. Says he gets all claustrophobic when shut in. Funny how he can be shut in the snug at *The Swan* and feel fine.
Bruce We must have a round of golf sometime, Andrew.
Andrew Sure, when I can fit it in.
Sandra Good-night, Andrew. Give my love to Ann when you write.
Andrew Will do.
Sandra And I'll return the tincture tomorrow. A fresh bottle.
Andrew No need.
Sandra Oh, yes, I will. One thing I can say about myself, when I borrow, I always return.

She gives Bruce a push and follows him out

Andrew calls a good-night from the front door, then returns. He moves swiftly now. He turns out the main lights and opens a drawer in the desk. He finds a torch, tries it for light. He switches off the desk lamp. At the fitment he pulls the woman's clothes from the cupboard and spreads them out on the settee. He realizes the handbag is missing and glances around, seeing it on the chair. He collects it and looks towards the archway, wondering if Sandra has seen this

Andrew Hell!

Returning to the settee and staying in his track suit he begins to dress in the woman's clothes. He will not get far before—

the CURTAIN *falls*

SCENE 2

The same. Saturday, midday

The window curtains are drawn back—winter sunlight. There is a tray of used breakfast things on the coffee table and a fresh pile of daily newspapers on the window sill, otherwise the room is as before

Voices are heard talking off in the hall

Joe Lipton is now seen as he carries two large suitcases beyond the archway

Lipton Shall I carry them up for you, Mrs Wingate?

Ann appears beside him

Ann No, my husband can do that later. Thanks for all your help, Mr Lipton.

She enters the room, carrying plastic carriers—two contain duty-free bottles, the third gaily wrapped gifts and an umbrella. She is dressed for travelling. She drops her flight and clutch bags on the window sill and takes the carriers to the settee

I feel quite guilty, asking you to give up part of your Saturday to come to my rescue.

Lipton (*putting down the cases in the hall*) That's OK. Glad I was in when you phoned.
Ann Can I—well, reimburse you for the petrol?
Lipton Not necessary. The van is covered by the school for petrol.
Ann In that case ... (*She takes a bottle from the carrier*) You and your wife can enjoy it with your lunch.

Lipton comes forward to accept the bottle

Lipton Are you sure? I don't like to——
Ann Please do.
Lipton Duty free?
Ann Of course.
Lipton Then thank you very much, Mrs Wingate. (*He takes the bottle*)

Sandra rushes in excitedly

Sandra Oh, you're back, you're back. I was making the beds and saw you from the window getting out of the van——
Ann Mr Lipton was kind enough to come and collect me from the airport. I couldn't get a taxi, some convention or other were grabbing all the transport.
Lipton I'll be off then, Mrs Wingate. The wife likes me to help her with the shopping on a Saturday. I'll close the door after me. (*He nods to Sandra and goes to the archway*)
Ann Thank you very much. I'm really grateful.

Lipton exits

Sandra (*waving at the air*) He always smells of garlic. Well, let me look at you. As glam as ever.
Ann I don't feel glam. I'm bushed. I need a shower and a couple of hours to get my bearings.
Sandra Back for good? No more dashing off and deserting us all? Oh, the coffee mornings haven't been the same without you.
Ann Still hives of iniquitous gossip?
Sandra Gossip, gossip, the very idea. We never say a good word about anyone! (*She giggles*)
Ann Plug in the kettle. I need a coffee now, strong and black.
Sandra I know, you want to avoid seeing the kitchen, and I don't blame you.

Sandra exits to the kitchen

Ann goes to the desk and dials

Ann (*on the phone*) Oh, hallo, is that Mr Corby ...? It's Jason Wingate's mother.... Good-morning.... I'm just back from New Zealand.... (*Smiling*) Yes, a wonderful holiday.... I was wondering, Mr Corby, if Jason could come home for the rest of the weekend? I could drive to Worthing after lunch and pick him up, if that's convenient?... Yes, I will see he's back at school by Monday morning.... No, don't tell him. I'd

Act I, Scene 2

like it to be a surprise. Fine. Thank you very much. Goodbye. (*She replaces the receiver*)

As she does, Sandra enters

Sandra I've plugged in the kettle and managed to find two clean mugs. Coffee won't be long.
Ann Thanks.

Sandra peeps into the drinks carrier on the settee

Sandra Wow! Who wants coffee when we have all this? We must celebrate your return. (*She selects a bottle*) Oh, great, Chablis. May I?
Ann Help yourself, but isn't it rather early?
Sandra Not for Chablis.

Ann sits while Sandra uncorks and pours out the wine

Ann Strange, you sit for hours on the plane doing nothing and then arrive at journey's end totally exhausted.
Sandra Jet lag. I had it after flying to Jersey. Andrew didn't know you were coming back today, did he?
Ann No, spur of the moment decision, thought I'd surprise him. There was a cancellation so I was in luck.
Sandra Good for you.
Ann I thought Andrew would be in but I couldn't get any answer when I rang so I called the school. He might have been there, catching up on some paper work; he sometimes does go in on a Saturday. Then Joe Lipton answered and said he'd fetch me.

Sandra hands her a glass of wine

Sandra Andrew's at the gym. I saw him this morning, jogging off in his track suit.
Ann I wanted to be back today. Our wedding anniversary. I bet he hasn't remembered.
Sandra Men seldom do. Many happy returns, anyway.

They clink glasses and drink

Ann I've brought him a gift, oh, and there are tokens for you and Bruce and Tris. I'll sort them out later.
Sandra Lovely, thanks. To be honest, Ann, we wondered if you intended to come back at all.
Ann It was a holiday.
Sandra A very long one.
Ann Yes, but then I hadn't seen my parents since they emigrated. And I also wanted to see New Zealand very much.
Sandra Hadn't you been there before?
Ann No.
Sandra As a travel courier I'd have thought you'd been everywhere.
Ann You go where you're sent. There isn't an option, it all depends on your languages.

Sandra Mine would be *bad language*. (*She giggles and tops up her glass*)
Ann French and Spanish and you're pigeon-holed. Of course I haven't worked since I married, apart from one summer when I did a stint as a London guide.
Sandra Enjoy it?
Ann Awful. You feel like a nursemaid with a bunch of recalcitrant toddlers. I had blisters and a permanent sore throat, shouting above the noise of the traffic: "Please, please, please, don't get lost." (*She pulls the umbrella from the carrier and marches up and down with it above her head*) A seasoned Pied Piper I was. (*Shouting*) Westminster Abbey, Houses of Parliament, The Tower, Downing Street, Highgate Cemetery ... "No, no, no, madam, there is no toilet here and if there is it's bound to be locked. No, no, no, sir, I wouldn't advise that, the tombstones are sacred on account of Karl Marx."

Laughing, she throws down the umbrella and holds her glass out to Sandra, who tops it up

I wonder why the Japanese always want old Karl. They fill their cameras with him and ask endless questions that I could never answer.
Sandra Anyway, I'm glad you're home, but you might have sent your "friends" postcards.
Ann I did send them.
Sandra Never got 'em. I said to Bruce: "Ann might desert Andrew but never Jason. She's devoted to her son."
Ann Why should I desert Andrew?
Sandra It happens. You could have met a dashing New Zealander and decided to link up with him, change of scene, change of heart.
Ann You read too many Mills and Boon. I was far too busy looking at the scenery to notice the men.
Sandra I'd have noticed. I could do with some real romance, some gorgeous male gazing into my eyes and being lyrical. Bruce gazes into my eyes and asks what's for supper.
Ann (*laughing*) Same Sandra, always short changing poor Bruce. He's a very nice man.
Sandra He's a very dull husband. You wouldn't know. Andrew's hardly dull, the macho, silent type. You never know what he's thinking, or doing for that matter. Secretive.
Ann Secretive? Why did you say secretive?
Sandra Well, he is. I came over here last night and he didn't want to open the front door. It was as if he had something to hide.
Ann What could he possibly have to hide?
Sandra How do I know? Draw your own conclusions.
Ann You've obviously drawn yours.
Sandra Well ... He's been very odd lately; he's out every night and I do mean every night, and you can't tell me he's always at the gym. They only meet twice a week and Saturday mornings, so where does he go?
Ann (*annoyed*) You've been keeping a close eye on him, have you? A thorough neighbourhood watch. Trust Sandra.

Sandra Don't get uptight. I'm your friend.
Ann I'll make the coffee. Calm us both down. (*She rises and goes to the kitchen door*)
Sandra All I'm saying is thank goodness you're back. Husbands shouldn't be let loose for too long. It's asking for trouble.
Ann What kind of trouble? Go on, you've said this much, say the rest. What kind of trouble?
Sandra I told you. He goes out at night. Where he goes I have no idea. It isn't my business.
Ann But you're making it your business.
Sandra Oh, God, why don't I keep my big mouth shut?
Ann Yes, Sandra, why don't you!

Ann exits into the kitchen, leaving the door open

Sandra I never seem to do anything right. When I try to be helpful it's thrown back in my face. (*Going to the kitchen door*) And another thing.
Ann (*off*) Yes?
Sandra There was a phone call when I was over here last night and Andrew snatched up the receiver and didn't give them a chance to speak. He said they had the wrong number and he was terribly angry.
Ann (*off*) Really?
Sandra You'll see a change in him. (*She wanders to the desk and flips open the file of cuttings*) It's all the trouble we've had, of course. It's got on people's nerves, made them edgy and—suspicious. Reporters about the place and the police asking questions. Mrs Barnaby was interviewed on television and we'll never hear the last of that. She imagines now she's a celebrity. I suppose they picked on her as she lives in East End Lane, near to Honeysuckle Cottage.

Ann enters and collects the tray from the table

Ann What are you talking about? Agnes Barnaby is in EastEnders?
Sandra No, no, she was interviewed for the media, standing at her kitchen sink. Mercifully, the camera focused on her microwave most of the time so we were spared her smug expression.
Ann It must be my jet lag. I'm not on your wavelength.

Ann exits to the kitchen with the tray

Sandra They had Agnes washing up the same cup ten times before they were satisfied. Then the camera showed the spot in the woods where they'd found the body.

Ann appears at the kitchen door

Ann Body! What body?
Sandra Don't you know? Didn't Andrew tell you when he wrote? We've had a murder!
Ann In West Lynstead?
Sandra Two hundred yards from your back gate!
Ann Oh, no!

Sandra A woman out walking her dog was raped and strangled.
Ann Who was it?
Sandra Not one of us. She was renting Honeysuckle Cottage for a holiday. Some holiday.
Ann Have they caught whoever ...?
Sandra No, they haven't. I've sent Tris away to my mother's. I'm not having her here with all this going on.
Ann Have the police no idea ...?
Sandra It doesn't look like it. They think it's a local man.

Ann stands shocked

And I think it's a local man, too. In fact I'm sure I know who it is.
Ann Who?
Sandra Our butcher.
Ann Oh, Sandy.

Ann exits laughing to the kitchen

Sandra You can laugh but he's got funny eyes. Of course we're having an extra lot of publicity because she was famous.

Ann comes to the kitchen door

Ann Famous in what way?
Sandra Dress designer. Not our league, we're more Marks and Sparks.
Ann I may have heard of her. What was her name?
Sandra Marion Ellis.

Ann shakes her head and exits to the kitchen

No family. Divorced. She had a dog, though. It was because of the dog she was out walking so late at night. They found it the next morning whimpering outside the cottage, still with its lead on; knew its way home all right, poor little thing. Miniature poodle. The vicar has taken charge of it until someone makes a claim. I'm surprised Andrew didn't mention the murder when he wrote to you, especially when he's so interested. He's kept all the newspaper reports.

Ann enters with two steaming coffee mugs

Sandra lifts up the file

See, all neatly cut out and dated. Very meticulous. When I came over here last night the room was festooned with papers, they were everywhere. He must order the lot, even the local rag. And here are today's. (*She points to the pile of fresh papers on the window sill*)
Ann Why were you over here last night? (*She hands Sandra a mug*)
Sandra Not to seduce your husband, if that's what you think. I had raging toothache and remembered you used to keep that tincture stuff. Not that it did any good. I had to go to the dentist first thing this morning and he's put in a temporary filling. I'm not supposed to drink anything too hot. Mind if I cool it?

Act I, Scene 2   15

Ann (*sarcastically*) I wish you would.
Sandra Thanks. (*She pours a generous measure of wine into her coffee*)

Ann goes to the desk and looks at the file

Still, I suppose Andrew could have other reasons for keeping those cuttings. Who knows? He's a dark horse, and he knew you'd be on his side, whatever he did.
Ann (*not listening but reading the cuttings*) What?
Sandra Stand by him through any eventuality ... loyal.

There is a knock on the front door

Expecting company?
Ann How could I be? No-one knew I was returning today. (*She looks from the front window*) It's a police car.
Sandra Don't panic, all in a day's round. They have to show willing so they pop in and out of houses as the fancy takes them.

Ann goes to answer the door

Sandra quickly adds more Chablis to her coffee

Voices are heard off in the hall. Ann returns with Evans

Ann My husband is down at the gym, I'm afraid. They're not on the phone there so I can't call him. Why did you want to see him?
Evans Just a word.
Ann Oh, this is my neighbour, Mrs Coburn. Inspector Evans, Sandra.
Evans *Chief* Detective Inspector Parry-Jones-Evans.

They shake hands. Sandra is intrigued

Sandra Oh, are you the new man from Scotland Yard? If so your reputation has gone before you.
Evans Has it indeed? How very embarrassing.
Sandra Oh, nothing unkind. They say you're a wizard. If anyone can solve our murder, you can.
Ann The *Chief* Inspector wants a word with Andrew.
Evans I'm a stranger in these parts. How far is this gymnasium?
Sandra No distance. You can walk it in ten minutes, jog it in five and drive there in three if there isn't a traffic jam, and with all the folks around our village at the moment, that's quite likely.
Evans My driver will find it.
Ann No, no, I'll fetch my husband, if you don't mind. On a Saturday morning he instructs young children; they could be disturbed, seeing the police car.
Sandra Not them. They enjoy all the razzmatazz.
Ann I'll be as quick as I can. (*She collects car keys from the hook on the fitment*) Look after the *Chief* Inspector, please Sandra.

Ann exits through the patio door

Evans moves forward and closes the door. He remains looking out

Sandra Mrs Wingate said to look after you. How would you like to be looked after, Inspector?

Evans This garden leads down to the woods then. Is there access?

Sandra Yes, Mr Wingate has built a gate at the end of his garden. You're not supposed to do that.

Evans No?

Sandra No. The woods are common land. Still, he's a law unto himself.

Evans Is he indeed?

Sandra Oh, yes, privileged. Headmaster. Important. Does what he likes, almost as good as being on the local council. (*She goes to the fitment and indicates drinks*) Feeling thirsty, Inspector? It'll be OK. They're not mean with the booze in this house.

Evans I wouldn't mind a small Scotch, as I have a driver out in the car. That is, if you're joining me.

Sandra Sure, I'll keep you company.

Evans This garden is not overlooked then?

Sandra (*pouring drinks*) That's right. Only house this side of the road. Oh, very private. You could sunbathe topless and not be noticed. If you've come to ask Mr Wingate to help with your inquiries you won't get much joy. He's very secretive.

Evans You live near here, Mrs Coburn?

Sandra Opposite. "The Firs." (*She hands him his glass and liberally pours wine into her coffee mug*)

He will not drink at all but moves restlessly about

Evans Did you know the murder victim, Mrs Coburn?

Sandra Know her? I don't think anyone knew her, not here in West Lynstead. The only time I ever spoke to her was outside the school.

Evans Yes?

Sandra Yes, I went to collect my daughter who'd had a music lesson from Andrew—Mr Wingate. He's the music teacher as well as headmaster, you see.

Evans A busy man indeed.

Sandra Anyway, Marion Ellis was standing by the gates as I drew up in the car. Odd, I thought, hanging about on a dark and bitterly cold evening like that.

Evans Waiting for someone?

Sandra Well, who? She didn't seem to know anyone in the village. So I thought I'd be friendly and introduce myself. I mentioned I was having a coffee morning the next day and asked her if she'd like to come.

Evans And did she? (*He walks the room, carrying his whisky glass but never drinking from it*)

Sandra (*sitting on the settee*) No, that's just it. She murmured something about, yes, she might and then Tris came out of the school with her flute and we drove off. When we reached the end of the road my daughter remembered she'd forgotten her homework books, so I turned the car and we went back. Mrs Ellis had gone.

Evans Given up waiting?

Act I, Scene 2   17

Sandra No, she'd gone into the school. Tris saw her in the hall speaking to the caretaker. She was asking for the headmaster's study. *The headmaster's study!*
Evans What was unusual in that?
Sandra Why should she want to see Andrew?
Evans It could be she knew him.
Sandra Yes, I've often wondered about that. Want topping up?
Evans No, thank you. But don't let me stop you.
Sandra I seem to have a real thirst today. (*She rises and adds to her coffee mug*)

While her back is turned Evans tips his drink into the plant on the window sill

Of course it's all the worry we've had. This keeps up our spirits. (*She giggles*)
Evans You were telling me about Marion Ellis. You had invited her to one of your coffee mornings. Did she attend?
Sandra No, she didn't. Well, I hadn't given her my address and I knew the holiday cottage wasn't on the phone so after dinner I drove over there. My husband was out so I had the car; he likes to walk everywhere when he can. My daughter was doing her homework with a friend so I had nothing better to do.
Evans So you saw Mrs Ellis again?
Sandra No, I didn't see her again. The lights were on in the cottage and the dog was barking, must have heard me drive up in the car. Honestly, I wish I hadn't bothered. I nearly wrecked our tyres on that rutted lane. Why anyone should want to have a holiday in a hideaway like that, I can't think.
Evans Mrs Ellis may have had her reasons.
Sandra I suppose so. Well, I knocked and rang the bell and there was no answer. I knew she was in all right, just didn't want to answer the door.
Evans Just wanted to be alone?
Sandra But she wasn't alone! I thought she might be having a bath or something so I lifted up the letter-box to call out my address and what do you think?
Evans Tell me.
Sandra A man was standing in the hall! A man—inches away from me.
Evans Did you recognize him?
Sandra How could I? I only saw his feet ... in black leather shoes. It was so eerie. Fast as I could I dived back in the car and drove off.
Evans Why was it eerie, Mrs Ellis entertaining a man in her cottage?
Sandra Don't you think so? When she wouldn't open the door to me? And she didn't come to my coffee morning, either. Then ten days after that she was murdered!
Evans Have the local police interviewed you and your husband?
Sandra What? (*Rather muzzy*) Oh, yes, routine inquiries they called it. (*She flops down on the settee and closes her eyes*) I didn't sleep a wink last night. Toothache.
Evans What does your husband do for a living, Mrs Coburn?

Sandra Do ... for a ... oh, we're in paint. Own a small business. Coburn Five Star, you may have heard of us. We never drip.
Evans Is the firm local?
Sandra What? Oh, no, it's in Pinehall ... seven miles from here. Bruce doesn't go in every day; as managing director he doesn't have to. Besides, he hates the smell of paint.
Evans When did your husband last go up to London?
Sandra No idea.
Evans (*consulting a miniscule notebook*) Then let me tell you. He went to London on the Saturday before the night of the murder.
Sandra Did he? Well, if he did ... are you sure he did?
Evans Yes, the fifteenth of October. He took a day return at the local station and, it would appear, came back from London very late.
Sandra I can't think why. It isn't as if he likes shows or sight-seeing. (*Suddenly evasive, sitting up*) Is it important?
Evans It could be.
Sandra Why? If he wanted to go to London on that Saturday, I don't see it's anyone else's business.
Evans You didn't know about it?
Sandra No. I was away for the weekend. Went to stay with my mother and took my daughter with me.
Evans He didn't tell you about it when you returned from your weekend?
Sandra (*jumping up*) Why should he tell me? Do you tell your wife everything? I bet you don't.
Evans I'll be along to see your husband later. Is he in?
Sandra No, he isn't. He's playing golf and he won't thank you for asking him a lot of stupid questions. And I don't see why you want to go around checking up on innocent people. Snooping. You're here to catch a murderer so go ahead and catch him and leave the rest of us in peace.
Evans This man at the cottage——
Sandra (*shouting*) I didn't recognize him. I told you I didn't. I only saw his shoes.
Evans Then it could have been anyone. Your own husband even?
Sandra (*hysterical*) Are you mad? My husband didn't know Marion Ellis.
Evans Are you sure?
Sandra Of course I'm sure.
Evans He doesn't tell you everything, you just said so. You also said he was out the evening you drove to the cottage. Did he tell you where he was going?
Sandra I don't remember. I expect he did. What does it matter? Oh God, my tooth's aching again.
Evans If your husband came off the last train on the night of the murder, then he would walk home through the woods. Yes?
Sandra I don't know. Sometimes he does and sometimes he calls at *The Swan* for a drink.
Evans All the pubs would have been closed that late and if he did go through the woods then that would have been about the time Marion Ellis was attacked.

Act I, Scene 2

Sandra, hands up to her face, is crying now

Sandra You've only been on the case five minutes and here you are accusing innocent people ... jumping to conclusions.
Evans I'm not accusing anyone—yet, Mrs Coburn.
Sandra Oh, yes, you are. I know your sort, all smiles and handshakes and taking a drink, pretending it's a social call and all the time trying to trip people up, force them into saying things they don't mean. (*She bangs down her coffee mug on the table. Shouting*) Well, my husband didn't kill that woman and I'm not going to answer any more of your questions because I don't bloody trust you! (*She rushes to the patio door as ...*)

Ann and Andrew enter. He wears his track suit and—important—his two-colour college scarf

Andrew Hey, steady on ...
Ann What's the matter?
Sandra Ask him. (*She points to Evans*) It's people like him who get the police a bad name. And if you take my advice you won't tell him a thing, not a bloody thing!

Sandra exits, crying loudly

Ann I'd better go after her.
Evans Yes, Mrs Wingate. The lady appears highly emotional. I do hope it was nothing I said.

Ann exits, closing the patio door behind her

Good-morning, sir. I'm sorry if I disturbed your Saturday work-out at the gymnasium.
Andrew We were just about through.

Evans offers his hand. They shake

My wife seemed to think it was urgent.
Evans No, no, not urgent, just a chat, feeling my way, you know. New boy to the district. Need people to help me over the stile, get me accustomed to village ways. I've always been a city man myself.

Pause. He looks pointedly at the drinks

If you're having a quencher I'll be glad to join you. It must be warm work at the gym.

He offers his empty glass. Surprised, Andrew takes it

Scotch please and neat.

Andrew pours out

Andrew So what can I do for you, Inspector?
Evans (*looking out the patio door*) You have a good view from here over the woods. It must put a substantial value on the property.
Andrew The garden is rather neglected.

Evans And why not? What time does a busy man like yourself have for a spot of weeding? You run the local school, I understand?

Andrew Yes, we cater for three other villages so we have a full complement of pupils, taking in junior and senior.

Evans returns from the patio and accepts his filled glass. He will not drink from it

Evans Thank you. Quite a responsibility.

Andrew I have a good team. Now I'm sure this isn't a strictly social call so if we can come to the point——

Evans I'm sure you want this unpleasant business cleared up as quickly as we do.

Andrew Naturally.

Evans You know at times I feel like a canvassing would-be politician, touting for votes. Nobody wants to see me on their doorstep; bit of an embarrassment I am.

Andrew You have a job to do.

Evans Yes, I'm glad you see it that way. Aren't you going to join me? I hate drinking alone.

Andrew (*hesitating*) I don't usually this early——

Evans Come on, you need a spot of relaxation.

Andrew pours himself a drink

It makes my day when I find someone co-operative. Mostly I meet with opposition.

Andrew Do you?

Evans Afraid so. Too close for comfort this murder. Now it's common knowledge that we're looking for a local man, people are inclined to draw their curtains, keep a low profile; better not get involved in case there's retaliation or worse, a friend they'd rather not blow on. You know, sir, it always amazes me this Neighbourhood Watch Scheme.

Andrew I thought the police were in favour.

Evans Oh, we are or would be if we thought you were serious.

Andrew What makes you think we're not?

Evans (*amused*) Well, sir, stickers on your windows frighten no-one away, apart from the flies.

Andrew Isn't that a cynical assessment?

Evans I daresay. Yes, I'm sorry. I'm being unfair. Any effort is better than none and why shouldn't you derive a sense of security from a window sticker?

Andrew You're contemptuous of our amateur efforts? Are you saying we haven't a hope in hell of catching or sussing out a real criminal—a murderer even?

Evans I'm saying, Mr Wingate, that your Neighbourhood Watch should occasionally focus on—the *neighbours* themselves. Killers come in all shapes and sizes, from all classes and they have to live next door to someone. (*After a pause*) Would your neighbours ever doubt you, sir? No

Act I, Scene 2   21

of course they wouldn't. How could they? A respected headmaster, trustworthy, dependable, beyond reproach. Do you mind if I sit down?

Andrew nods to a chair

Thank you. Trouble with leg veins ... all the years on the beat, takes its toll. (*He sits*)
Andrew Can we get down to business? If there is any business, that is.
Evans Did you know Marion Ellis, sir ... personally, I mean?
Andrew (*after a slight pause*) I had seen her. Any stranger in the village is conspicuous.
Evans I said *personally*. Did you ever speak to the lady?
Andrew Yes, I did. She came up to the school once.
Evans To see you?
Andrew To see the headmaster, actually. The caretaker brought her to my study one evening. I was late on the premises as I had been conducting a music lesson.
Evans Yes?

Andrew gulps down his drink

Go on, sir, the lady came to your study?
Andrew Mrs Ellis was enquiring about adult evening classes.
Evans How extraordinary. The lady was on holiday and only renting Honeysuckle Cottage for a limited time.
Andrew Was she? In any case I had to tell her we weren't having evening classes this winter.
Evans I see. I'll change gear if I may, sir. (*He opens his notebook*) I wonder if you can tell me the time of the last train down from London on a Saturday night?
Andrew They can tell you that at the station.
Evans Indeed they can and have. I was there this morning ... spoke to that Dickensian character, Ted ... Ted what?
Andrew We don't know his surname. He's just Ted. A railway institution and master of all he surveys.
Evans Every village should have one.
Andrew Every station has got one, it seems. Our Ted should have retired years ago, but he's kept his age under lock and key.
Evans You don't like him?
Andrew We tolerate the man. He has an in-built dislike of the travelling public. A necessary qualification for the job, it appears. Now and again he likes to get above his station ... sorry. Anyway, why are we talking about Ted?
Evans He was talking about you this morning. Whatever his other shortcomings, he has a retentive memory for faces. He remembers, for instance, who buys day returns and who are the regular commuters with season tickets.
Andrew I'm not exactly *au fait* with this particular inquiry ... last train, our Ted, day returns. Where is this taking us?

Evans It's something the local police here have kept under wraps. I won't be using a loud-hailer myself. This information is strictly for those whom it may concern. In fact, Mr Wingate, those who bought a day return ticket to London on the fifteenth of October.

Pause

Andrew I did.
Evans Yes, we know you did. What train did you return on?
Andrew The last. It gets in at around midnight.
Evans And you gave up your ticket—the return half—to Ted at the barrier?
Andrew No, I was the only passenger at this station. I came over the bridge and there was no-one in the booking hall.
Evans So you kept the ticket, pocketed it?
Andrew No, I left it on the shelf in front of the closed booking office. I always do that if there's no-one to collect.
Evans For once you may have forgotten, sir.
Andrew If I had it would have been in my pocket, and when I came in I emptied out everything, including loose change. If the ticket had been there I'd have seen it.
Evans I suggest the ticket wasn't in your pocket when you came in because—you had lost it ... *lost it on the way home*!
Andrew No, I left it on the booking office shelf. It's a natural reflex action, something I've done many times. There's seldom anyone around that late to collect.
Evans Ted has told me he was still on duty that night but couldn't flag out the train and collect any tickets as he was busy in the toilet. The small matter of a stomach bug. But he insists that when he did surface there were no tickets left, and for that reason he assumed there'd been no passengers.
Andrew Too bad. I did leave the return half.
Evans Did you take a short-cut home through the woods?
Andrew Of course. I always do when I come off the train.
Evans Did you meet anyone?
Andrew No.
Evans Hear anything?
Andrew Nothing.
Evans Yet Mrs Ellis was murdered just about the time you were supposedly passing through the woods. But you claim you saw nothing, heard nothing.
Andrew Good God, Inspector, the woods are dense, they cover a wide radius. I understand from reports Mrs Ellis was found in undergrowth, right away from the main path.
Evans And you kept to the main path?
Andrew Yes, the one that brings me out at my garden gate.
Evans (*looking at his notebook*) The forensic people have given the time of death at between eleven and one o'clock. That would give anyone coming from the last train ample opportunity, wouldn't you say?
Andrew If you say so.

Act I, Scene 2   23

Evans Why is it you haven't chosen to tell the local police about your movements that night?
Andrew They didn't ask me.
Evans And you didn't volunteer the information?
Andrew Why should I? There was no way I could assist them.
Evans Yet you were right there in the vicinity. No-one could have been closer to Mrs Ellis that night.
Andrew (*furiously*) Except the murderer!
Evans As you say, sir ... *except the murderer*!
Andrew What the hell is this? Are you insinuating that whoever did this crime, *must* have travelled by train that night?
Evans It narrows the margin.
Andrew Why?
Evans Because a day return ticket was found in Bracken Woods. We know it could not have belonged to Mrs Ellis since she had spent the whole day in Wrenstock, taking a taxi there and back.
Andrew All right, so a ticket was found. It could have been dropped anytime, anywhere. What possible significance can it have on this murder?
Evans This ticket when found ... was on the dead woman's body!

Pause

Are you still telling me, sir, you left your return half on the booking office shelf?
Andrew Yes, I bloody am and if Ted told you otherwise, then he's lying!
Evans Why should he lie?
Andrew He's supposed to collect the tickets and didn't, and for another reason——
Evans Another reason?
Andrew He's waging a personal vendetta against me.
Evans Is he now ... for what reason?
Andrew (*restless, walking the room*) There was some trouble last Christmas.
Evans Yes?
Andrew He accused my son of vandalizing a chocolate machine on the station. I know the boy didn't do it but that didn't stop Ted. He savagely beat Jason with a walking-stick and I was flaming mad. I went to see Ted and—thumped him.
Evans A violent man?
Andrew I was provoked.
Evans An unfair advantage, surely? An elderly station porter would be no match for you.
Andrew And my ten-year-old son was no match for a thug with a heavy walking-stick.
Evans You could have prosecuted. Instead you took the law into your own hands. You prefer to do that, work on your own, play judge and jury?
Andrew I felt I had every right. If Ted wanted to prosecute me, he could have done so. I'd have welcomed that.

Evans Before we get any deeper into the mire, Mr Wingate, let's straighten ourselves out. How would Ted know it was *your* ticket that was left on the shelf, if indeed it was.
Andrew (*confused*) He may not have been in the toilet as he claims. He could have been in the booking office with the hatch down. He can still see out, he has a spyhole. Possibly there were many tickets he didn't collect that night and he was covering himself.
Evans They have checked at head office. All the day returns for that date were accounted for ... save one.
Andrew God, Inspector, you're chasing moonbeams. Stop wasting my time and your own with this crackpot inquiry and stop listening to half-wits like Ted. I left my ticket on the booking office shelf and I don't intend to discuss it further.

Ann enters through the patio door and stands listening

Evans In that case we'll leave it there ... for the time being. Ah, Mrs Wingate, I hope your neighbour is herself again?

Ann nods

Good. I was just leaving. (*He looks at his glass*) There now, didn't have my drink after all. Never mind, it will keep until next time. (*He rises, puts down the glass and smiles*) I'm glad we've had this friendly chat, Mr Wingate. Thank you so much for being ... helpful.
Ann I'll see you out.

Evans follows Ann to the archway, then pauses

Evans If anything else occurs to you, sir, jogs your memory, you know where to find me. I'm staying in the village for the present, at *The Black Swan*. (*Speaking to Ann as he walks out*) They've made me very comfortable.

Evans and Ann exit to the front door

Alone, Andrew flings a cushion to the floor and kicks it

After a pause Ann returns

Ann What did he want?
Andrew Checking.
Ann On what?
Andrew It isn't important.
Ann Sandra was upset. I think it was something the Inspector said about Bruce.
Andrew Can we forget him and Sandra? Happy homecoming, darling. (*He holds her*) I wish it had been less traumatic.
Ann So do I.
Andrew You should have forewarned me. I'd have put a stop on it.
Ann Didn't you want me to come home?
Andrew Naturally. But not in the present climate. Better to have stayed in New Zealand until the circus has moved on.

Act I, Scene 2   25

Ann Murder is hardly a circus, Andrew. (*She moves away from him*)
Andrew Some imagine so. Can't wait to get in on the act.
Ann It's horrible. (*She shivers*)
Andrew Sure, but then horror and all its grisly off-shoots have a certain attraction, don't you think? Our dull old village spotlighted, on the map at last, pivot of interest nation-wide. Switch on the telly news any evening and the odds are you'll see a reporter in duffle coat, bleary-eyed from too much Bell's booze at *The Black Swan*, standing piece-to-camera, filling in the country on the latest hot-line from dreary West Lynstead.
Ann Don't.
Andrew Or maybe they'll picture our prize reporter outside my school. Yes, why not? That'll pull a spot of emotion. Mums scurrying past with offspring and looking over their shoulders for the benefit of camera. You've seen it all before, my love. (*He helps himself to a drink*) They're just re-enacting the regular old spools. Can't you hear the news director screaming for some more nitty-gritty information. "What have you got for us tonight, lads? The dead woman's dog is always good for a tearjerker ... show the poor blighter in the vicar's garden, peeing up against the rose bushes."
Ann Oh, Andrew!
Andrew If you think that's spreading the sentiment too thick, let me tell you, Ann, that endearing little frame was on the box a week ago and later we were told a hundred and seventy-four viewers phoned to adopt the little orphan doggie.
Ann That was kind of them, surely?
Andrew Think so? Then forgive me if I'm cynical. That was the dog the woman was walking when she was raped and strangled. He's a macabre celebrity in his own right.
Ann You're taking all this too personally.
Andrew Sure. Let's forget murder and those who enjoy the limelight and go out for an anniversary lunch.
Ann So you have remembered?
Andrew I sent flowers to you in New Zealand.
Ann Thank you, darling. Mother will enjoy them.
Andrew Shall I ring the *Griffon*, see if we can have our favourite table? I rather fancy Sole Veronique. There's nothing much here, apart from a few out-dated fish fingers.
Ann I can't go out to lunch. I'm driving to Worthing to collect Jason. I rang the school and his housemaster said he could come home for the rest of the weekend.
Andrew Oh, no!
Ann Why not? I haven't seen my son for three months.
Andrew Jason stays away until the decks have been cleared. Now make up your mind, woman, what'll it be? The *Griffon* or fish fingers and an afternoon under the duvet?
Ann What a generous man you are. But I do quite fancy fish fingers.
Andrew Good. (*He kisses her lingeringly*) Just a teaser to remind you how it is.

Ann Miss me?
Andrew Like hell. A lonely bed and electric blanket cannot compensate.
Ann I didn't mean to stay away so long. Dad wasn't too well and Mother needed my support.
Andrew I need your support now you are back.
Ann Can you take my luggage upstairs?
Andrew Will do, lady, but get those fish fingers going. I'm starving. (*He goes into the hall to collect the luggage*)
Ann I brought you back a present.
Andrew Something I want or need?
Ann Need.
Andrew Then it has to be socks.

He is seen with the two large suitcases crossing the hall to the stairs. He exits

Ann unloads the bottles from the carrier bags. She opens the cupboard in the fitment, bends down and slowly draws out the woman's clothes. Amazed, she straightens up, gazing at them

Andrew enters

(*As he enters*) Any more to go aloft?

He pauses, watching her as she holds out the clothes

Ann What's all this?
Andrew Gear.
Ann Woman's gear and not mine. Have you been entertaining while I've been away? Have you, Andrew?
Andrew Don't get upset.
Ann Who is she? And why has she left her clothes behind? What was it, a quick strip down here, couldn't wait to satisfy yourselves upstairs? A lonely bloody bed indeed! Who the hell do you think you are kidding? (*She drops the clothes and kicks out at them*)
Andrew Calm down and listen. I can explain.
Ann You might have had the decency to dispose of this sleazy lot before I returned.
Andrew (*joining her*) I'm not disposing of them (*He pauses*) They're mine.
Ann Oh, for God's sake. I've heard some choice excuses men make when caught out, but this——
Andrew They were purchased in Pinehall where I'm not known ... purchased from a charity shop. The lady was very helpful, searched through her stock until she found what would fit me.
Ann *Fit you?*
Andrew Your wardrobe couldn't accommodate, darling. Nothing large enough. I told the charity lady I was an actor in need of gear for a drag act. (*He returns the clothes to the cupboard*)
Ann (*sitting, shocked*) A transvestite and I never knew. What else don't I know about you?

Andrew My idiosyncrasies don't stretch in that direction. I dress up and go out for a purpose.
Ann You go *out in woman's clothes*?
Andrew At night and every night.
Ann You could be seen!
Andrew That is the *raison d'être*. I *want* to be seen ... *and attacked*!
Ann Who's going to attack you?
Andrew The murderer, I hope. That's what I'm waiting for. That's my objective and why I keep my lonely vigil. In the past week, since I had this brainwave, I've become very familiar with those woods. Often I'm frozen stiff and on wet nights soaked to the skin; it's a small price to pay. The wild life tolerate me, they know I wish them no harm and consider I'm part of their habitat now.
Ann What's it all for?
Andrew Bait for a killer.
Ann Bait——?
Andrew I'm convinced our local killer will strike again and when he does, *I* want to be the target.
Ann Why should he take the chance of being out there again?
Andrew Because he's local and this particular swine knows his territory, every path and copse, every twist and turning. Plenty of undergrowth and trees to shield him, and once successful, then the magnetic pull exerts itself again, so back to the same happy hunting ground for another victim.
Ann Don't the police mount their own patrol there?
Andrew Oh, they have an occasional skim through; make plenty of noise, flashing their torches, voices calling to one another. I've heard 'em and so has he if he's there.
Ann What do you do when the police are around?
Andrew Carry on, look as if I'm a nervous female hurrying home, taking a short-cut through the woods.
Ann Suppose they stop and question you? Your disguise could be blown. It wouldn't be the first time a crazed killer has dressed as a woman. Christ, Andrew, you could be erecting your own gibbet. The police could think you murdered Marion Ellis.
Andrew Yes, I have considered that possibility.
Ann And still you take the risk? Still, you go out there——?
Andrew I have to get him, Ann, and when I do ... I'll castrate the bastard!
Ann God almighty!
Andrew Why not? Doesn't he deserve it? What mercy did he show Marion Ellis and what mercy will he show the next victim who falls into his evil clutches?
Ann *You* could be his next victim. How can you always be alert, on your guard, out there night after night without sleep——
Andrew I take a few cat-naps in my study at school, the door locked, blinds down. To all intents and purposes I'm working on next year's curriculum.
Ann (*furious*) Stop this, Andrew, stop it before it's too late! This monster could get you, jump you from behind, murder you even ... then there'll be another body for the mortuary!

Andrew Trust me.

Ann Well, I don't. You're too damned confident and you have no feelings for Jason and me when you're ready to risk so much; your job, your reputation, even your life, playing cowboys and Indians on a wild escapade. This is a job for the professionals, so leave it to them. You're not cut out to be a vigilante.

Andrew I'm sorry, Ann, but there's no room for debate. I have to get him. (*He pauses*) You see, I think I know who he is.

Ann (*rising*) Then what are you waiting for? Ring the police.

Andrew What proof, what evidence? If I make an open accusation then I must substantiate my claim and I can't do that. Not yet.

Ann Who is it? Who do you suspect?

Andrew Not even to you, darling, am I going to make a fool of myself. I have to be a hundred per cent sure ... and sure I will be one fine night when the devil comes at me.

Ann (*going to him*) You're paranoiac and you're dicing with death. *Your death!* You've been badly affected by this murder, so badly it's as if a member of your own family were involved.

Andrew (*nodding*) Could be.

Ann And the only way you can come to terms with the situation is by entering into the whole horrific business. Why does it matter to you so much? Why, Andrew, for God's sake?

He turns away, shrugs

Murder happens all the time, yet you feel some moral obligation to catch the killer personally. Tell me why? I have to know, Andrew, otherwise I can't stand by you.

Andrew (*calmly*) Not to worry. If it doesn't pan out my way and he gets me before I get him, I have taken the necessary precautions.

Ann What precautions?

Andrew A letter has been lodged with my solicitor, only to be opened in the sad event of my demise. "The corpse names his killer!" How's that for a spot of sensationalism? The Sunday tabloids will love it.

Ann You're enjoying this. Yes, you are. You want to be top of the class, star pupil, hero in the mudpile. Your photograph flashed across the front of newspapers. (*She points to the file*) Leave a few blank spaces in that so that you can be included. (*With heavy sarcasm*) "The hour produces the man. Headmaster beats the professionals, performs the ultimate ... neighbourhood catch!"

Andrew Yes, why not? Slay the dragon before he slays again. But I won't slay him. I'll bring him in alive, if I get the chance. I'll shower now and be down in fifteen minutes. Pop the fish fingers under the grill, my love, and I believe there's a spot of Stilton in the fridge. Awash with wine we'll have a banquet.

Andrew exits to the stairs

Ann moves to the desk and studies the file of cuttings. The phone rings

Ann (*as she lifts the receiver*) Hallo, Mrs Wingate speaking. ... (*Her expression registers horror*) What do you mean? ... Who are you? ... Marion Ellis and my husband. ... They knew each other?

Andrew enters, running

Andrew (*shouting*) Put it down!
Ann He says—he says you and Marion Ellis were at her cottage and that—you were lovers.

Andrew tries to wrest the receiver away. She hangs on tightly

No, I want to hear what he has to say ... I want to hear. Let go.

Andrew, furious, pulls the cord from the wall plug

Andrew The bastard won't make any more filthy, lying calls to us!
Ann (*still holding the dead receiver*) You did know her, you did. That's why you're so involved, so interested. Why you've kept all those bloody cuttings and a large printed blow-up of her photograph.

He stands motionless, breathing heavily

Were you in love with her. Were you?
Andrew Yes. Once.

Ann flings down the receiver, brushes past him, snatches up her flight bag and handbag

Ann I'm going to Worthing to be with Jason. I'll be back on Monday afternoon ... to discuss the divorce.

She exits through the archway to the front door

Angrily Andrew swings away from the desk, picks up his scarf and knots it into a noose

CURTAIN

ACT II

Scene 1

The same. Monday evening, 6 p.m.

The Lights are all on. The phone is still disconnected. The newspapers have gone, as have Andrew's scarf and the female clothes from the cupboard. Andrew's anorak lies on the chair in the hall

Ann enters through the archway with Melody, who is in school uniform, with a whistle around her neck on string. She carries a recorder and a "Walkman", the headset clamped over her ears

Ann I'll tell Mr Wingate you're here. He's upstairs watching the news on television. Was he expecting you?
Melody (*lifting up one earphone*) Eh?
Ann Was he expecting you?
Melody Oh, yeah. Said to be here at six, sharpish.
Ann To have a music lesson?
Melody Yeah.
Ann He doesn't usually hold music lessons at home. Have you been here before?
Melody No. (*Curious, she stares about her. She claps the earphones back on*)
Ann What did you say your name was?
Melody Eh?
Ann (*loudly*) Your name? I asked you your name? I didn't catch it at the front door.
Melody Melody.
Ann Appropriate if you're studying music.
Melody Eh?
Ann I think you'd be able to hear me if you took off the headset. (*She points to it*)

Melody pushes the headset down to her neck

Oh, you're learning the recorder, that's interesting.
Melody I'm not any good.
Ann It's a question of being keen.
Melody I'm not keen. I just want to get into the school orchestra and you can't unless you play something.
Ann That's logic.
Melody Tone plays the drums. He's really good. He can make more noise than anyone.
Ann Your boy-friend?

Act II, Scene 1   31

Melody Yeah, he's going to start a group when he's seventeen. It's going to be called "The Little Drummer Boys".
Ann Unusual.
Melody Yeah. Tone's got ideas, wants to get on.
Ann Are *you* ambitious, Melody? What are you going to do when you leave school?
Melody Be a Page Three Girl!
Ann *(turning away, amused)* My son would like to be a professional musician. He plays the violin.
Melody Oh, yeah.
Ann Yeah ... I mean yes! I've been to see him this weekend. I stayed at an hotel and he and a friend were allowed to come out with me.
Melody What you do?
Ann Well, we went for drives, visited a maritime museum and a stately home.
Melody Nothing exciting, then?
Ann Oh, I don't know. We had meals in a restaurant and went to a concert on Saturday evening. Classical music, of course.
Melody *(grimacing)* Reads music, does he?
Ann Jason? Yes, don't you?
Melody No. *(She wanders the room restlessly)*
Ann I'll tell my husband you're here. I won't be a minute. Sit down.

Ann exits through the archway to the stairs

Melody claps on the headset and reacts to what she is hearing, rocking around and doing a wiggle as if at a disco. She picks up an ornament, nearly drops it and, scared, quickly replaces it. Then she snatches up a cushion and uses it as a partner. She should never be still

Ann returns

Melody drops the cushion back on the chair and pushes down the headset. She sits

He'll be a couple of minutes. He just wants to see the end of a news item.
Melody About the murder, is it?
Ann I—don't know.
Melody Shall I come back later?
Ann No, he wants you to wait. Would you like a drink ... Coke, bitter lemon, squash?
Melody No, thanks. I've just had me tea.
Ann Shall I find you a magazine?
Melody I see enough mags in the shop.
Ann Oh, of course, your father runs the newsagents in the village, doesn't he? I thought I'd seen you somewhere before. You serve behind the counter occasionally.
Melody Yeah, worse luck!
Ann Don't you enjoy it?

Melody Dead boring. I have to do a paper round in the mornings if one of the lads don't show up. I'm always getting it wrong. The vicar did his nut when I pushed *The Sun* through his letter-box.
Ann (*smiling*) Your father pays you for working for him, surely?
Melody Peanuts. He thinks I should be glad to help out for me keep and clothes.
Ann How old are you?
Melody Fourteen—*and five months*!
Ann Aren't you happy at home?
Melody They're always at me. Bad as bloody school—oh, sorry.

Andrew enters from the archway, formally dressed

Andrew I didn't hear that, Melody.

Melody leaps up, hands behind her back with respect

I didn't think you'd be so punctual but I'm glad to see you are. Ann, do you think we could have some coffee?
Ann Melody didn't want a drink.
Andrew Then can I have a coffee, please?
Ann (*nodding*) Is it going to be a habit, holding music lessons at home?
Andrew The exception is not the rule.

Ann exits to the kitchen

(*Pointing to the armchair*) Over here, please.
Melody I like to stand when I'm playing.
Andrew You won't be playing. This isn't a lesson.
Melody You said——
Andrew I know what I said. I wanted to see you alone and in private.
Melody You could have seen me in your study at school, sir.
Andrew My study is never private enough. And turn off that contraption, I can hear it grinding out a cacophony of rubbish. If you're going to learn a musical instrument you'll need to listen to good music.
Melody This is *good* music, it's "Top of the Pops"!
Andrew (*sharply*) Turn it off and sit down.

Melody does so. She sits and sniffs

Have you got a cold?
Melody Shouldn't be surprised.
Andrew I shouldn't be surprised, either. Too many late nights out of doors ... out of doors—in Bracken Woods.

Melody reacts, startled

You were there on Sunday night and alone near that vandalized seat on the main footpath. Why?
Melody I never saw you, sir.
Andrew Why were you there, Melody, and what were you doing? Waiting for someone?

Act II, Scene 1

Melody shrugs

(*Shouting*) Were you waiting for someone?
Melody (*sniffing*) Maybe.
Andrew You children have been set a curfew by the school: off the streets after seven at night and never, ever to go into Bracken Woods. How many times do you have to be told?
Melody (*sulkily*) You can't rule us out of school hours.
Andrew This is for your own good, can't you understand that or are you too stupid or stubborn to appreciate the danger? We have an unsolved murder on our doorsteps and until the monster is caught, women and children must be vigilant and use common sense.
Melody I didn't know I was asked to come here for a lecture. It's as bad as school—nag, nag, nag.
Andrew In that case I won't lecture or nag. I'll just inform your parents.
Melody (*leaping up in fear*) Oh, no, sir, no, please don't.
Andrew So your parents had no idea you were out last night?
Melody No, course they didn't. My dad would kill me if he knew. I'm sent to bed at nine just as if I'm a bloomin' kid.
Andrew You are under the control and jurisdiction of your parents and they have a right to know what you are doing and where you are at all times, and sneaking out of the house when they imagine you are in bed is disloyal and cheating on their trust. Sit down!

She doesn't

(*Shouting*) Sit down.

She does so sharply

Now are you going to tell me why you were in the woods or would you rather tell the police?
Melody (*startled*) The police? What the hell has it got to do with the police if I want to meet Tone——? (*She claps a hand to her mouth*)
Andrew Is that it... Tony Bishop from the school, the lad you hang around with? Is that who you were waiting for last night?
Melody No, I wasn't. Tone doesn't know nothing about all this and if he did he'd give me the send off; he doesn't like any kind of hassle. His last girl got the shove when her mother started making trouble. Tone says it's not worth the candle if there's going to be any fuming.
Andrew So you weren't waiting for Tony Bishop? Then who were you waiting for?
Melody How do I know? He didn't give his name and address, hardly do that, would he? He just left a note at the shop.
Andrew A note?
Melody Yeah. It's good it was Sunday or my dad might have seen it. Dad sleeps in late Sundays and I have to go to the station for the papers. When I got back the note was there, shoved through our letter-box.
Andrew Delivered by hand?
Melody Course. No stamp nor nothing.

Andrew Where is this note?
Melody I burnt it.
Andrew Oh, my God!
Melody I couldn't risk my dad finding it.
Andrew The writing could have been a clue.
Melody There wasn't no handwriting; just words cut from newspapers. Must have taken him all night.
Andrew What did the note say?

Melody shrugs

What did it say?
Melody That I had to meet him in Bracken last night at eleven sharp.
Andrew And?
Melody Be on the broken seat and take five quid in coins.
Andrew Blackmail?
Melody Yeah. I didn't have that much so I had to borrow it from the till. (*Defiantly*) And I've never done nothing like that before. Never taken anything from the shop, except Pick 'n' Mix. Tone likes Turkish Delight.
Andrew Why did this character think he could blackmail you? What have you done?
Melody Nothing.
Andrew So why did *you* imagine you could be blackmailed?
Melody He might have seen me the night before with Tone. We were only fooling around under the trees, but my dad wouldn't have worn that. He's got a dirty mind.
Andrew Don't be so disrespectful. So like a stupid fool you went along in answer to that note?
Melody I had to go or he'd have split on me. I reckon it's a kid from the school. They'll do anything for ciggy money.
Andrew You knew those woods were a no-go area at present.
Melody Where else can Tone and I meet? Not his place or mine and they've taken away that old crock of a Ford on the rubbish dump.
Andrew So this character saw you and young Bishop on Saturday night *in flagrante delicto*.
Melody Eh?
Andrew He must have recognized you in order to leave that note on Sunday morning?
Melody Everyone knows me as I work in the shop weekends.
Andrew You should have taken that note straight to the police.
Melody They'd have told on me.
Andrew So instead you'd run the risk of meeting a killer—face to face?
Melody No, no, no, you've got it all wrong, sir. It's a boy from the school, like I said, and I was going to give him a piece of my mind if he had shown up.
Andrew And if he had there would have been one less at assembly this morning. *You*, Melody.
Melody I'm not scared of the louts at school. I can give 'em as good as I get any day of the week and they know it. Besides, I've got me whistle. (*She

shows it on a string around her neck) I'd have blown it like mad if anyone had come at me.
Andrew You are still convinced it was a lad from the school?
Melody Yeah, I am. I mean, who else would be so barmy, spending hours cutting bits from papers to make up that note? He might just as well have written it 'cause I was going to recognize him and could have told on him later, if I wanted to.
Andrew If you'd been *alive* to tell!

She shivers

Listen to me, Melody, listen to me carefully. There's a killer about, a local man. Yes?
Melody So they say.
Andrew He has already raped and strangled once and, given the opportunity, would like to repeat the crime. A young girl, completely defenceless, could easily arouse his sadistic appetite and be his next victim.
Melody But it wasn't *him* that left the note.
Andrew No? Then allow me to disillusion you. In my opinion that note was compiled and delivered by the killer!

Melody covers her face with her hands

I don't want to alarm you, but it seems I must to ram the message home. No female is safe in this locality until that man is caught. Now I want your solemn promise that you will not enter Bracken again until the curfew is lifted. Understood?

She nods

Melody Can I go now?
Andrew Yes, but I want no mention of this conversation relayed to anyone, and that includes Tony Bishop. In fact I think it would be better if you stopped seeing the lad, out of school hours.
Melody (*shocked*) I can't stop seeing Tone. If I did he'd back off and go with someone else. A lot of the sixth form fancy Tone. He wouldn't have far to look.
Andrew It's an order, Melody, and unless you want your parents informed of your nightly activities, you will obey me. I'll get the car out and run you home.
Melody I've got me bike. (*Tearfully*) Tone's OK, sir. Tone would never harm me or anyone. Why can't I see him?
Andrew We've struck a bargain. Tony Bishop is off your scene for the present or your parents will be brought in. They have a right to know what their daughter is doing and who she is seeing at night.
Melody It's bloody blackmail!
Andrew Blackmail—for your own good.

Melody is crying loudly as . . .

Ann enters with a mug of coffee

Ann What's the matter?

Andrew The child is learning a hard lesson. It's known as self-preservation.
Ann She's upset, Andrew.
Andrew She'll be more upset if she doesn't do as she's told.

Ann puts down the coffee mug and goes to Melody, slipping an arm around her shoulder

Melody (*sobbing*) He says ... he says I can't go out with Tone and I must. Tone is all that matters to me.

Andrew goes to the desk and empties the contents of his briefcase

Andrew The girl is leaving, Ann. Will you see her out, please?
Melody (*as she is led through the archway*) I love him, I love him. I can't live without Tone, and if he gets someone else I'll die — yes, I will, I'll die, I'll die.

Melody, still crying, exits to the front door with Ann

Andrew takes his empty briefcase to the fitment

Ann returns

Ann Was that necessary? Why can't she see her boy-friend?
Andrew Never mind.
Ann Do you have to be so pompous and overbearing? If so keep it within school hours. I don't like scenes like this in our home.
Andrew I'd appreciate an early meal, is that convenient? I have a parent-teacher meeting this evening.
Ann Yes, sir, anything you say, sir.
Andrew I have children all day, Ann, I'd prefer not to reason with one at home.
Ann You've changed.
Andrew Really?
Ann Yes, really. It's this damned murder!
Andrew Have you seen my scarf? I thought it might be in my briefcase but it isn't. I had it this morning when I walked to the school.
Ann Then that's where you've left it. What about the phone? Is anyone coming to fix it?
Andrew We'll leave it on hold for the time being.
Ann So what am I supposed to do without a phone?
Andrew Use Sandra's.
Ann And have my every call carefully monitored?
Andrew Just for the present. Are you coming to the meeting? Good if you put in an appearance, showed an interest as you've been away so long.
Ann It seems I haven't been away long enough.
Andrew We'll be discussing the Nativity Play. Perhaps you'd like to produce it.
Ann No, thanks.
Andrew The parents give up time, involve themselves, so why can't you?
Ann Because I'm not village orientated. For years I've tried to be what you want, the dutiful headmaster's wife, always available for any chore no-

Act II, Scene 1   37

one else wants to take on board. I'm stifled, claustrophobic. When the highlight of my week is one of Sandra's ghastly coffee mornings, then I know there's something wrong with my mental state. Well, if you won't have the phone re-connected, I will. First thing tomorrow morning.

Ann exits to the kitchen

Andrew goes to the fitment and opens the cupboard door. He searches inside and realizes the clothes are missing

Andrew (*calling*) Ann, have you seen my gear?

She enters and stands at the door

Ann What did you say?
Andrew My gear. Everything was back in that cupboard last night.
Ann I've burnt the lot.
Andrew Bloody hell!
Ann When I returned from Worthing this afternoon I had a bonfire. (*She goes to the patio door*) If you want the evidence you can see it for yourself. The ashes are at the end of the garden.
Andrew You had no right——
Ann I had every right. I can't live with this, Andrew, and I won't. What you've been doing is sheer madness and highly dangerous and I refuse to be part of it.
Andrew I was going to discuss it with you over the weekend, but you chose to do a disappearing act.
Ann I wasn't in the mood for a confession of guilt.
Andrew You were upset after that filthy, lying call.
Ann Why should anyone ring with that monologue unless it's the truth?
Andrew Would you like the truth? Or would you prefer to fantasize as no doubt you've been doing all over the weekend. If you promise to stay calm we can talk this through rationally.
Ann Rationally? There isn't a wife alive who'd cheerfully accept that her husband was having an affair behind her back.
Andrew All right ... I did have an affair with Marion.
Ann I see.
Andrew It was before I met you. Marion and I were close friends at university and we intended to marry later, once our careers had got going. (*He walks about restlessly*) Then I met you and it was an explosion.
Ann You never told me about her.
Andrew Why should I? It was on my conscience so why should it be on yours?
Ann So you jilted her?
Andrew Yes, to marry you. At the time she took it well; that's the kind of person she was.
Ann And all these years you've been seeing each other, meeting secretly, salving your conscience by deceiving your wife? The way you men reason it all out.
Andrew I hadn't seen Marion for years. She married eventually and divorced eighteen months ago. She became ill, went into a nursing home

and then happened to hear a broadcast I made on education. She wrote to me through the radio station.

Ann And that started up the whole love story all over again?

Andrew I didn't answer her letter. But somehow she discovered where I was teaching and took that holiday cottage. Had you been home we could all have met and tried to help with her problems. She was a very sick lady, Ann, and she needed a friend.

Ann So you proved to be that friend. A shoulder to cry on? Convenient, wasn't it, that your wife was thousands of miles away?

Andrew Stop this, stop being jealous of a dead woman, a murdered woman! Murdered because she came to this village to see me and ended up in Bracken, raped and strangled. How the hell do you think I feel about all this?

Ann If you didn't ask her to come here, then it wasn't your fault.

Andrew It was my fault. Christ, Ann, have you any idea what I've been going through these past two weeks? I've had to hide my grief, suffer alone the intolerable pain, bury my conscience, pretend no more interest than a complete stranger, and all the time I've been feeling as guilty as if I'd killed Marion myself. So don't tell me it isn't my fault. That woman wouldn't have been in those woods or this village if it hadn't been for me. (*He collapses into a chair and buries his head in his hands. He is emotionally upset*)

Ann pours a drink and takes it to him

Ann Did you go to her cottage?

He nods and downs the drink

Staying the night?

Andrew We talked; we talked for hours. If you want to believe otherwise then I can't stop you but it's the truth.

Ann How many times did you meet?

Andrew I didn't keep a ready reckoner. Three, four times. What the hell does it matter? We were discreet.

Ann I wonder.

Andrew Then go on wondering, go on being jealous of a dead woman if it gives you satisfaction. I once let Marion down badly and I owed her at least some of my time. In all the years we've been married we've never doubted each other, Ann. Do we have to doubt each other now?

Ann That anonymous phone call——

Andrew Oh, yes, I've had quite a few from that evil devil. It must have been a bonus hearing you on the line.

Ann You mean he knows me?

Andrew He knows us both.

Ann I didn't recognize the voice.

Andrew You wouldn't. He's adept at disguising it then pours out the filth.

Ann Why? What's the point?

Andrew He wants me to go to the police, report the calls; it's all the mischief of a diseased mind.

Act II, Scene 1   39

Ann And you haven't reported the calls?
Andrew No, I prefer to play this according to my own rules.
Ann But don't you see this makes you more of a suspect than ever? Marion Ellis, an old flame, comes to this village and tries to invade your private life. You meet secretly and then in sheer desperation, because she's becoming a burden and an embarrassment, you—you——
Andrew Murder her?
Ann The police could assume that. Please, Andrew, please keep out of Bracken Woods in future.

A knock at the front door

Andrew Whoever it is, get rid of them.
Ann (*looking from the window*) I can hardly do that. It's the police.
Andrew Not the Welsh tenor again, for God's sake.
Ann Perhaps he's returned to finish his drink.

Ann exits to the front door

Andrew closes the cupboard door and takes his briefcase to the desk

Ann enters with Evans, who is talking

Evans Chilly out, shouldn't be surprised if we don't have snow before long—ah, good-evening, sir. I hope I'm not intruding.
Andrew I am rather rushed for time.
Evans Aren't we all?
Ann My husband has a meeting at the school this evening.
Evans Always on the job? Conscientious to the letter, now that's what I appreciate. Never off duty for long, just like we are in the Force——
Andrew I'd be grateful if you'd come to the point of this visit, Inspector.
Evans Yes, indeed. I was wondering if I could have your passport.
Andrew Why?
Evans Just a formality.
Andrew I'm not *going* anywhere.
Evans Then you won't object.
Andrew Oh, no, I won't object. (*He opens the desk drawer and pulls out his passport*) Help yourself.

He flings it towards Evans who has to pick it up

Ann Why do you want my husband's passport?
Evans Observing the old red tape. We would also appreciate it if you'd come along and make a statement, sir.
Ann What about? My husband isn't accused of anything and he's told you all he knows.
Evans A few more pointers we would like cleared up.
Andrew When do you want me to come?
Evans Now, sir, if it's convenient.
Andrew Well, it isn't bloody convenient. The meeting is at seven-thirty and I haven't eaten yet.

Evans We have a good canteen, can rustle up sandwiches. (*To Ann*) Our sandwiches are very good, Mrs Wingate. I should know, I've been living on them myself all over the weekend.
Andrew Are you arresting me?
Evans No, no, sir, nothing so tiresome.
Andrew So I can refuse?
Evans It wouldn't be in your best interests.
Ann You'd better go, Andrew.
Evans Wise lady.

Ann collects Andrew's anorak from the hall and hands it to him

Andrew Why is this necessary? I can answer any questions here.
Evans A new development has come up. We need your full co-operation and we'd like you to give a statement and sign it.
Andrew What new development?
Evans We can discuss it all at the Incident Room. Don't worry, sir, (*he taps his watch*) I'll personally see you make the meeting on time.
Andrew I'm not leaving here until you tell me why you want an official statement.
Evans (*his manner changing to one of aggression*) Were you in Bracken Woods last night?
Andrew Yes.
Evans For what purpose?
Andrew Looking for conkers!
Ann Andrew!
Evans Shall we go, sir?
Andrew I want to know and my wife has a right to know ... what new development?
Evans I was hoping to spare Mrs Wingate any embarrassment but as you insist ... We received a phone call half an hour ago. It was from a very frightened and distressed lady. She said she had been trying to pluck up courage all day to ring us and kept putting it off out of fear. She didn't give her name but promised to call again and I hope she will.
Andrew Some anonymous caller and you take that seriously?
Evans We have to keep our options open, sir. If this is a serious lead then we must follow it up. The lady insisted she had been raped and attacked in Bracken soon after midnight.

Ann and Andrew exchange glances

    She said she recognized the man by his voice, although he was hooded.

Ann slowly sits down. Pause

    The lady was in no doubt at all that the man ... was *you*, Mr Wingate.

CURTAIN

Scene 2

The same. Later that night

The hall and living-room are fully lit. The car keys are on their hook. A coffee pot, two mugs, a cheesecake and a large knife (important) are on the coffee table. Classical music is playing. Ann is seated at the desk, reading the cuttings file

After a pause, there is loud knocking on the front door

Sandra (*off, calling through the letter-box*) It's only me. Open the door.
Ann (*sighing*) All right, coming.

Ann exits to the hall and returns with Sandra who has "dressed up" for the parent–teacher meeting

Sandra I knew you were up when I saw the lights. Where's Andrew — gone to bed?
Ann He isn't back from the meeting yet.
Sandra Not back? He left ages before the rest of us. I was going to offer him a lift as I knew he hadn't his car but I couldn't find him. Oh, turn off that thing.

Ann turns off the record

Ann You've no soul. Sit down. The coffee's hot. Like some?
Sandra I don't mind.
Ann You can use Andrew's mug, as he isn't here yet. (*She pours coffee*)
Sandra (*sitting*) I wonder if he went back to police headquarters?
Ann What?
Sandra They could have released him for the meeting on the understanding that he reported back to them. Let him out on bail.
Ann Don't be stupid, Sandra.
Sandra (*taking her coffee mug*) Well, he was taken into custody earlier, wasn't he? We saw the police car outside here.
Ann Then you sat diligently at your window, awaiting further developments? Oh, Sandra, you never change.
Sandra No point in having a Neighbourhood Watch sticker on your window if you don't watch out.
Ann You carry it too far.
Sandra Bruce said it looked as if they were arresting Andrew, but I said: "No, they couldn't be. They didn't bring him out with a blanket over his head."
Ann (*laughing*) Have a slice of cheesecake.
Sandra Oh, lovely, home-made?
Ann No, I bought it on the way back from Worthing.
Sandra On second thoughts, no, dear. Better not. I've started at Weight-Watchers so it's tuna fish for me from now on.

The cake remains uncut

So why did they take Andrew away?

Ann They didn't take him away. He went voluntarily. Does Bruce know you're here?

Sandra He's out. Don't ask me where. He refused to come to the meeting and when I went in just now—gone.

Ann He's probably at the golf club. The bar stays open late and they play bridge occasionally.

Sandra Yes, could be. Mind if I give them a buzz and see? (*She rises and goes to the desk*)

Ann Our phone's out of order.

Sandra How come?

Ann I caught the lead in the Hoover. Come and sit down.

Sandra So where's my husband and where's Andrew? (*Restless, she walks about*)

Ann We can't impose a curfew on husbands. The men can look after themselves.

Sandra looks from the front window, lifts the curtain

Sandra Still dark over the road, so he's not back yet. Where the hell is Bruce? Don't you worry, Ann?

Ann No, should I?

Sandra Bruce isn't the only one who likes night prowling. If I were you I'd be suspicious. Doesn't anything ruffle you?

Ann Oh, yes, plenty.

Sandra God, my nerves are in ribbons. That damned Inspector Evans called on us yesterday—imagine, a Sunday with a police car outside the gate. I can't think what the neighbours thought.

Ann What did Evans want?

Sandra Asking a lot of damn fool questions. I didn't sleep a wink last night. I kept wondering why Bruce had gone up to London on the day of the murder and why did he walk home through the woods?

Ann Didn't you ask him?

Sandra Evans did that and Bruce shrugged, said he thought he'd bought a tie in London. But he hasn't got a new tie.

Pause

Was Marion Ellis strangled with a tie?

Ann Sandra, stop this!

Sandra Well, how do I know if Bruce had anything to do with the murder? How does anyone know? They keep saying it's a local man ... someone's husband!

Ann Bruce is hardly the type ...

Sandra Then who is the type? Is it tattooed all over them? "I'm a rapist and killer." Be a bloody sight easier if it were. Andrew went up to town the same day, you know.

Ann Yes.

Sandra Bruce saw him on the platform in the morning.

Ann rises and leads Sandra to a chair

Act II, Scene 2

Ann Tell me about the meeting—how did it go? Boring as ever?
Sandra Hardly that. It was fine at first, then suddenly all hell was let loose.
Ann Why?
Sandra We were just discussing the Nativity Play when the door burst open and that man Bishop charged in.
Ann Bishop? Tony Bishop's father?
Sandra He was dragging young Tony with him by the collar and you could see the lad was scared out of his wits and been brought along against his will.
Ann Tony is Melody's boy-friend. She was here earlier this evening.
Sandra I've never seen anything like it. Old man Bishop was purple in the face, shouting and swearing and making a scene. I thought he'd have a seizure or break up the place, and the temper he was in, it's a wonder he didn't.
Ann What was all the fuss about?
Sandra From what we could gather Bishop had come in from the pub and caught his son with a couple of friends watching a video nasty.
Ann That's hardly the responsibility of the school.
Sandra It appears Tony told his irate father that's where he'd found it, on the school premises.
Ann Oh, no!
Sandra Andrew tried to calm everyone down and hold the meeting together but he didn't succeed. Then Tony got away from his father and rushed up to the platform and whispered something to Andrew. The next thing we knew Andrew snatched up his anorak and tore out. No explanation or even a good-night.
Ann I wonder why?
Sandra We all wondered that. It was sheer chaos. Then that bitchy Mrs Cathcart said Andrew couldn't stay and face the music and must be a coward.
Ann Andrew never runs out on anything.
Sandra Well, he did tonight, believe me. And when I looked for him afterwards to give him a lift home. Gone.
Ann And all over a video nasty? Kids are always watching them.
Sandra This was very bad, it seems, the most horrific thing Mr Bishop said he'd ever seen; brutal and sadistic.

Loud banging on the patio door

Good God, who's that?

Ann goes to patio door and draws back the curtain

Don't answer it. You never know——
Ann It's Melody. (*She unlocks the door*)

Melody staggers in. Her clothes are dirty, her face streaked with mud and she is gasping. Round her neck is Andrew's scarf

What's the matter, what's happened?
Melody Don't let him get me, don't let him, don't let him!

Ann closes the patio door and puts her arm around Melody

Ann No-one's going to get you.

She leads the sobbing girl to the settee and sits her down

Fetch some water, Sandra. Quickly, please.

Sandra nods and runs into the kitchen

It's all right, dear. Calm down, you're quite safe now.
Melody I had to come here, the nearest house to the woods.
Ann Is that where you've been, in Bracken?
Melody Oh, God, I thought I was going to be strangled by—by this. (*She points to the scarf*)
Ann (*shocked*) That belongs to my husband.
Melody He came at me with it and—kept tightening it. It was like a noose. (*More sobbing*) I thought I was going to die. I could hardly breathe. Then—then he dragged me into the bushes and—and knocked me to the ground. Oh, it was terrible, terrible ...

Sandra enters with a glass of water

Sandra How is she?
Ann She's been attacked in the woods.
Sandra Oh, no, not raped?
Ann (*taking the water*) Phone the police, Sandra.
Sandra But your phone's out of order.
Ann From your house.

Melody leaps up

Melody No, no, you can't. I don't want the police. They mustn't know. No-one must know about this. My parents think I'm at home and in bed and my dad will kill me if he finds out.
Ann No-one's going to kill you. Now sit down and drink this.
Melody (*pushing the water aside*) I don't want the police.
Ann Your parents will understand.
Melody You don't know my dad. You don't know what a temper he's got. He'll say it's all my fault.

Ann sits Melody down

Ann Take it easy, everything will be all right.
Melody And Tone will get into trouble, too, and he never did anything, except ask me to meet him.
Ann Tony Bishop—you were meeting him tonight in Bracken?
Melody I had to see him. I phoned him and told him what Sir had said, that we couldn't see each other out of school; Tone told me to meet him by the seat in Bracken and we'd talk it through. (*Sobbing*) I waited and waited and he didn't show up.
Sandra He couldn't meet you, Melody, he was dragged to the school by his father. Forced there.

Act II, Scene 2

Melody (*not listening*) I don't think Tone loves me any more, he can't do to leave me stranded like that. I was so cold and frightened. Then—then this figure came at me. Oh, it was awful, Mrs Wingate. Awful. He dived from behind the trees like a wild animal and he jumped me, and he had this scarf——
Sandra That's Andrew's scarf!
Ann Yes, it is. Will you please, please Sandra, ring the police ... tell them a young girl has been attacked in Bracken and is here now, so will they come at once.
Sandra You heard what the girl said. She doesn't want the police.
Ann Never mind what she wants. Move, Sandra. (*Shouting*) Move!

Sandra nods and goes out through the archway to the front door

Ann sits beside Melody and unwinds the scarf

(*Gently*) Was it my husband ... was it, Melody?
Melody I don't know. I don't know who it was. He was disguised, hooded, all in black. And he was mumbling ... sex talk, oh, it was horrible.
Ann Did you recognize the voice?
Melody No, it was all croaky and slurred and he kept tearing at my clothes ... oh, God, I'll never, ever forget it.
Ann You did manage to get away, you have to be thankful for that.
Melody I wouldn't have done if I hadn't got the whistle. I kept blowing it and blowing it. I thought if Tone comes he might hear the whistle and save me. (*Suddenly*) Perhaps it was Tone ... who came up, I mean, and dragged the beast off me. Oh, yes, yes, get the police, perhaps it's Tone out there ... they were fighting and I crawled away and then I stood up and ran. Oh, Mrs Wingate, if Tone's out there fighting the man he could get hurt. Tone's big and strong but he might not be able to ... Oh, why did it have to happen to me?
Ann You should never have gone into Bracken. But we won't talk about that now.
Melody I must look awful. I ought to clean myself up. I wouldn't want Tone to see me looking like this.
Ann You can use the bathroom upstairs.

Ann leads Melody to the archway. They pause as ...

The patio door crashes open and the hooded man in black, (Joe Lipton), blunders in, gasping

Melody screams and races to the stairs and exits

Ann stands motionless, horrified

Andrew, slightly breathless, enters through the patio door. He pushes the hooded man on to the chair by the kitchen

Andrew Phone the police from across the road.
Ann Sandra is doing that now. Melody is here—upstairs.
Andrew Go to her, Ann.

Ann No, I'm staying with you.
Andrew I don't want you in the same room as this—scum.
Ann I have to know what's going on——
Andrew (*standing over Lipton*) Yes, cringe, you bloody coward. You enjoy terrorizing women and school kids, but when it comes to a man-to-man you squeal for mercy.
Ann Who is it?
Andrew Let's find out, shall we? (*He drags back the hood*)
Ann (*gasping*) Joe Lipton—the school caretaker! I don't believe it.
Andrew Then you'd better believe it.
Ann He's always so polite, so mild. He came to the airport and helped me with my luggage.
Andrew Christ, Ann, if you'd known the danger you were in. (*To Lipton*) What new heinous scheme was fermenting in that malevolent brain of yours? Bring the headmaster's wife home, get into the house with the luggage then while you were both alone here . . . another victim, easy prey.

Ann stands petrified

(*To Ann*) He knew I was at the gym and as usual would stay out to lunch. He could have carried your body upstairs and hidden it and it could have stayed concealed all day and I wouldn't have known . . . when you were found who else could possibly have murdered you . . . only your husband?
Ann But Sandra ran in while he was here. Oh, thank God for Sandra.
Andrew (*to Lipton*) Those porn videos weren't enough to satisfy your sadism; your Marquis de Sade tendencies needed more exciting nourishment. You wanted to act out the deeds, indulge in the ultimate kill to reap the bloody satisfaction you craved. (*To Ann*) But there had to be a bonus . . . a fall guy, and he hated me because I knew too much about his dirty private activities. I suspected he went to dog-fighting matches when I discovered monstrous photographs at the school. When I challenged him he swore they weren't his, but I knew he was lying.
Ann Why didn't you report the matter to the governors?
Andrew (*to Ann*) It was pity for his poor damned, abused wife that stopped me. They'd have lost their home and the job and there'd have been no references, so for her sake I didn't report it. (*To Lipton*) But you no longer felt safe, did you, after our confrontation? And your cunning brain figured out a way to get back at me. You had brought Marion Ellis to my study and latched on to the idea that we were old friends. She may even have told you we were and that put a diabolical scheme into your crazed thinking. (*To Ann*) He knew Marion walked her dog late at night in Bracken and he lay in wait for her that Saturday. He imagined I'd be suspected of the murder, as I was the only local man who knew the lady. (*To Lipton*) Then after the killing you went to the station to make sure of your own alibi. You knew old Ted, a drinking crony, would back you up and say you'd been together for hours, if necessary.
Ann You're only surmizing this, Andrew.
Andrew Sure I am. (*To Lipton*) But it's the truth, isn't it? Only your plan misfired. Ted was missing and that threw you. You hung around in the

shadows, thinking the old fool might return to see the last train in. He didn't show up but I did, the lone passenger off the London train who left his ticket on the booking office shelf. Once I'd gone you snatched that ticket and followed me. By then Marion Ellis was dead and I saw nothing as I walked home through the woods. After that, it was easy, wasn't it, to put the ticket in a conspicuous place for the police to find?
Ann He thought your prints would be on it?
Andrew Yes, I wasn't wearing gloves but he made sure he was. Only it rained heavily later that night and the prints were obliterated.
Ann How did you know he was at the station—did you see him?
Andrew No, but I smelt the garlic breath and knew he was close. I didn't know why then; it was only later, after I knew about the murder, that I started to piece it all together and the picture fell into place. He made those vicious, accusing phone calls, hoping I'd report them to the police and so put myself in their eye-line.
Ann But you didn't report them?
Andrew No, and he found that hard to fathom. (*To Lipton*) I dressed as a woman to snare you and many times I knew you were in Bracken, drawn back to the scene of your bloody crime and anxious for the next victim. I hoped, prayed, you'd attack me.
Ann Yet he didn't. Could he have recognized you in spite of the clothes?
Andrew Perhaps he'd like to tell us? Well, Lipton?

Lipton stares ahead

Too damned scared to speak. In any case he wanted a girl from the school. (*To Lipton*) You had seen Melody in the woods with her boyfriend and that gave you the idea to deliver the blackmailing note to the newsagents. You wanted to entice the girl alone into Bracken on Sunday night and like a fool she went. But there were too many people around so you had to abandon that plan. But tonight was the night. (*To Ann*) He had stolen the scarf from my study and my guess is he had seen Melody going into the woods. This was his chance and, by God, he meant to take it.
Ann Melody strangled with *your* scarf? What better damning evidence? You'd have been arrested for—double murder! (*She turns away and covers her face with her hands*)
Andrew (*to Lipton*) Evil takes all forms and yours reaches the depths of depravity. As for your poor, pathetic wife, what pressure did you put on her to make that call to the police, accusing me of attacking her? That we'll never know unless she can be persuaded to give evidence against you and perhaps she will, glad to be free of you at long last.
Melody (*calling, off*) Mrs Wingate ...
Andrew Take the girl back upstairs, Ann.
Ann Will you be all right ...?
Andrew Please go, Ann.

Ann nods and exits to the stairs

So it's all over, Lipton, the frightened rat trapped at last before the final act of treachery could be accomplished. Long may you rot in jail, you devil.

Lipton rises and dives for the cake knife on the table. He lunges at Andrew and they battle for a few moments. Then Andrew twists Lipton's hand behind his back and the knife falls to the floor. Andrew flings Lipton back on to the chair and picks up the knife

I vowed when I caught Marion's killer I'd castrate him. So why don't I? (*Shouting*) Why don't I, Lipton? Or shall we leave it for your future prison mates to get you . . . they enjoy a target, and a sex fiend is never safe from their clutches.

The sound of police cars approaching in the street, sirens screaming. The sirens continue. Hammering on the front door

Ann is seen crossing the hall to open the door

(*Yanking Lipton to his feet*) Sounds as if they've called for you in style.

He frog-marches Lipton into the hall. Voices are heard off

Ann enters and picks up the scarf

The sirens cease blaring

Andrew enters with Evans

Citizen's Arrest, Inspector. My privilege.
Evans Then I have to thank you for your assistance, sir.
Ann More than assistance, surely? You come along with three cars and a load of men. My husband managed this alone. If he hadn't been in Bracken Woods tonight you'd be investigating the murder of a schoolgirl. (*She holds out the scarf*) This is what the monster was trying to strangle her with. You may need it as part of your evidence. I doubt if my husband will have any more use for it.
Evans (*as he takes the scarf*) Where is the girl?
Ann Upstairs. She's still very frightened.
Evans She'll have to come along for questioning.
Ann We'll bring her in our car. I'd like to be with her when she faces her parents.
Evans We'll need a statement from you, too, sir.
Andrew After I've had a drink. (*He pours himself a drink*)
Evans How were you in the right spot at the right time, sir?
Andrew Tony Bishop had arranged to meet the girl in Bracken and when he was prevented from doing so he had the sense to warn me. He was anxious because he knew she was alone. Our caretaker, Lipton, was missing and that set up alarm bells.
Ann My husband has always suspected him of the Ellis murder, Inspector.
Evans Really? In that case he should have informed us.
Andrew I had no solid proof and I rather thought you'd laugh in my face— the amateur fictional detective.

Act II, Scene 2   49

Evans We never laugh. We listen. Occasionally.
Andrew I had to be sure. Thank God Melody was able to blow her whistle and thank God I heard it. I was two hundred yards away and I ran like bloody hell.
Evans Right, sir, I'll see you in the Incident Room.
Ann Sure you don't want a drink, Inspector?
Evans (*smiling*) No thank you. I never drink ... on duty.

Evans exits to the front door

Ann I'll get my coat and bring Melody down.

Andrew touches her arm

Isn't any risk too great for you?
Andrew It didn't quite work out as I planned, only I had to get him, Ann. Thank you, darling, for believing in me.
Ann I'm not sure I always did. One thing I do know ... I never stopped loving you.

He kisses her

She smiles and goes out to the stairs

Andrew finishes his drink. At the desk he picks up the file of cuttings, holds it for a moment, then drops it into the waste-paper basket. He takes his car keys from the hook, turns out the room lights. He stands facing front in the archway, silhouetted only by the hall light

CURTAIN

FURNITURE AND PROPERTY LIST

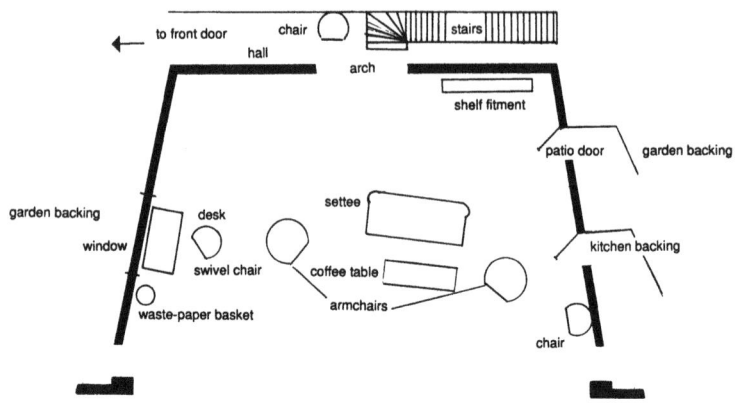

ACT I

Scene 1

On stage: Settee. *On it:* cushions, newspaper cuttings, scissors
2 armchairs. *On them:* cushions
Coffee table. *On it:* tray with remains of Chinese take-away meal
Shelf fitment. *On it:* bottles of drink including Scotch, glasses, corkscrew, record player with record on turntable, books, records, hook with car keys, lamp, ornaments. *Below it:* drawer, cupboard
Desk. *On it:* telephone with long lead, lamp, large red file. *In drawer:* torch (practical), passport
Swivel chair
Waste-paper basket
Chair. *On it:* long black skirt, glitzy jacket, gloves, blonde wig, handbag with shoulder strap over back of chair
Carpet
Window curtains (closed)
Patio door curtain (closed)
Neighbourhood Watch stickers on windows and patio door (with key)
Large potted plant on window sill
Mangled newspapers scattered round room

Murder in Neighbourhood Watch   51

	In hall: Chair Carpet
Off stage:	Mug of coffee (**Andrew**) Bottle of toothache tincture (**Andrew**)
Personal:	**Andrew**: wrist-watch

Scene 2

Strike:	Coffee mug Dirty glasses
Re-set:	Female clothes and handbag in fitment cupboard Window and patio door curtains open Tidy cuttings file on desk
Set:	Fresh daily newspapers in window sill Tray with used breakfast things on coffee table
Off stage:	2 large suitcases (**Lipton**) 3 plastic carriers, 2 with duty-free bottles of wine, 1 with wrapped gifts and umbrella; flight bag; clutch bag (**Ann**) 2 mugs of coffee (**Ann**)
Personal:	**Evans**: small notebook, wrist-watch (required throughout)

ACT II

Scene 1

Strike:	Umbrella Andrew's scarf Female clothes from cupboard Dirty glasses and mugs Empty wine bottle Plastic carriers and contents Newspapers
Re-set:	Empty waste-paper basket Cushion on settee
Set:	Andrew's anorak on chair in hall Briefcase containing papers by desk
Off stage:	Recorder (**Melody**) Mug of coffee (**Ann**)
Personal:	**Melody**: whistle on string round neck, "Walkman" personal stereo with tape and headphones (practical)

Scene 2

Strike:	Briefcase Dirty glass and mug

Re-set:	Cuttings file open on desk
	Window and patio door curtains closed
	Patio door locked, key in lock
Set:	Pot of coffee, 2 mugs, cheesecake on plate, large knife on coffee table
Off stage:	Glass of water (**Sandra**)
Personal:	**Melody**: whistle on string round neck

LIGHTING PLOT

Practical fittings required: wall-brackets, desk lamp, lamp on fitment, light in hall
Interior. A living-room. The same scene throughout

ACT I, SCENE 1   Late evening

To open: Fitment lamp on, hall light on

Cue 1	**Andrew** switches on desk lamp *Snap up desk lamp*	(Page 1)
Cue 2	**Andrew** switches on main lights *Snap up wall-brackets*	(Page 2)
Cue 3	**Andrew** switches off main lights *Snap off wall-brackets*	(Page 9)
Cue 4	**Andrew** switches off desk lamp *Snap off desk lamp*	(Page 9)

ACT I, SCENE 2   Morning

To open: General interior lighting—winter sunlight

No cues

ACT II, SCENE 1   Evening

To open: All lights on

No cues

ACT II, SCENE 2

To open: All lights on

Cue 5	**Andrew** turns out room lights *Snap off all lights in living-room, leaving hall light on*	(Page 49)

EFFECTS PLOT

ACT I

Cue 1	As CURTAIN rises *Classical music plays*	(Page 1)
Cue 2	**Andrew** switches off music *Cut music*	(Page 2)
Cue 3	**Sandra**: "... I never break a promise." *Telephone rings*	(Page 4)
Cue 4	**Ann** moves to the desk and studies the cuttings file *Telephone rings*	(Page 28)

ACT II

Cue 5	As SCENE 2 opens *Classical music plays*	(Page 41)
Cue 6	**Ann** turns off record *Cut music*	(Page 41)
Cue 7	**Andrew**: "... never safe from their clutches." *Sound of police cars approaching, sirens screaming—continue sirens*	(Page 48)
Cue 8	**Ann** enters and picks up the scarf *Sirens cease blaring*	(Page 48)

www.ingramcontent.com/pod-product-compliance
Ingram Content Group UK Ltd.
Pitfield, Milton Keynes, MK11 3LW, UK
UKHW021848210426
53221PUK00022B/529